Studies through the Book of Genesis

Origins

Chapters 1-11

From the Bible-Teaching Ministry of

Stephen Davey

Rough-edited Manuscripts
© 2004; Reprinted 2012, 2014, 2016 & 2021. Stephen Davey, All rights reserved.

My thanks to Lisa Bright, Gary Ellis, Pam Shelton and Vince Smith for converting these dusty sermon manuscripts into something readable and usable for Bible students and teachers alike.

Unless otherwise noted, all Scripture quotations are taken from the
New American Standard Bible ®,
Copyright © 1960,1962,1963,1968,
1971,1972,1973,1975,1995 by The Lockman Foundation
Used by permission. (www.Lockman.org)

Production by Tailored Text

———————————————

Wisdom International
2703 Jones Franklin Road, Suite 105
Cary, NC 27518

Origins

Genesis 1-11

The Book of Beginnings

Genesis 1:1

Introduction

Why should we attempt to study the entire Bible?

Today we are going to begin by laying a foundation as to the reason we are to embark on this kind of journey. Let me give a couple of reasons why we study the Bible in its entirety.

The Bible is entirely true

The first reason that we are to study the entire Bible is because the Bible is entirely true.

There is no doubt that in our American society in the last ten to twenty years, there has been a battle raging as to whether or not the Bible is entirely true. If you have assumed that I believe the Bible is entirely true, you have assumed correctly. And because we do believe that all of the Bible is the word of God; all of it is true; all of it is without error, we will study it in its entirety.

Reasons the Bible is entirely true

Now, there are several reasons why I believe that the Bible is entirely true. Let me give them to you.

Fulfilled prophecy

What does the Bible say about itself? If I were asked today, the primary reason I consider the Bible to be true, I would suggest immediately – the fulfilled prophecies of scripture.

We already know from previous studies that there are at least three hundred prophecies alone that prophesy the coming of Jesus Christ – His birth, His life, His death, His resurrection, and His ascension. Three hundred prophecies have already come true. They were written, of course, before the time of the events, so we consider them prophetic. More than one quarter of the Bible, when it was written, was prophetic.

Now, we all pick on weathermen. Sometimes they predict that it is going to rain and instead, it is sunny. Then we are happy. Sometimes they say it will be sunny and instead, it rains. Then we are not happy.

The Old Testament criteria for a prophet was that he had to always be correct – one hundred percent of the time. In fact, the Old Testament records in the book of Deuteronomy that if a prophet was ever wrong, he was assumed to be a false prophet and was taken out of the city and stoned. Now I am not suggesting we do that to the local weatherman, but you need to understand that the people would not have any confidence in the prophet unless he was always correct.

There was also a certain thing that the prophets had to do. If they declared themselves to be a prophet of God, they first had to prophesy something that was to happen in the near future in their city and among their people. If that prophecy came true, then the people would trust them for a prophetic event to take place in the years to come.

For instance, Micaiah, a prophet we are told of in I Kings, chapter 22, told King Ahab that if he went to battle as he planned, he would not only lose the battle, but he would lose his life. Ahab's false prophets told him another story – that if he went to battle, he would win. And of course, Ahab being the humble man that he was, decided to believe the false prophets. He had Micaiah thrown in jail, telling the guardians to give him only bread and water until he returned from battle safely and victoriously. Micaiah's words in I Kings 22:28 were,

... If you indeed return safely the Lord has not spoken by me..

We know from the Old Testament recordings, that Ahab indeed lost the battle. The scripture says not only did he lose the battle, but as the battle was nearing an end, an enemy soldier took an arrow from his quiver and shot it at random into the air. It had Ahab's name on it. So, as the battle was coming to a close, this soldier at random; that is, "I have one arrow left, so why not?" just plunged that arrow into his bow and shot it. It finds Ahab and kills him.

We know then that the prophet Micaiah was a prophet of God.

Today, there is the question, and in fact, I have been asked this more than any other, "Are there prophets living today? Are there people receiving revelation today?"

Turn in your Bible for a brief answer to this question, before going on to another passage. Look at Hebrews 1:1, 2. It is as clear as the nose on your face that there is no such thing as a prophet living today and receiving revelations from God, whether it is one who claims to know Christ or one from another religious belief system, because Hebrews writes,

> *God, after He spoke long ago to the fathers in the prophets in many portions and in many ways, in these last days . . .*

(Did you notice the phrase, "in these last days"? The prophets are past tense, but the "in these last days" is in the present tense. So, how has He spoken to us?),

> *. . . has spoken to us in His Son, whom He appointed heir of all things, through whom also He made the world.*

So, if someone suggests that there are prophets today, they are in opposition to the clear writing of scripture – that the prophets are past tense and that in the present tense, we have the living word and the written word of Jesus Christ. That is the revelation from God to us.

Ladies and gentlemen, may I suggest to you that if God would break the sound barrier and speak today, He would repeat something that He has already said. One of the reasons I think the Bible is entirely true is because of fulfilled prophecies.

Its Preservation

This is an objective proof, but it is marvelous. Jeremiah tells us of one occasion when the king was handed a copy of the Old Testament writings and he took a knife, cut it into pieces, and threw it into the fire (Jeremiah 36). That attitude has come down through the centuries and even today, men outlaw Bibles from our schools, they attack and would outlaw the Bible from our courts, they attack and would outlaw the name of God from every institution in our land. They are still attacking this Book and yet, God miraculously continues to preserve His word.

I have in my library, a copy of two ancient manuscripts that go back to the time of John the apostle. There is no one who would question the writings of Homer and yet, you have to go more than a thousand years past the time of Homer before you find a manuscript of his writings. God's word goes all the way back to the time of the apostles. And from that time to this, God has miraculously preserved it. Although men have burned thousands of copies; although men have outlawed it; although men have tried to stamp it out, God has preserved His word.

Before we leave this point, may I suggest to you that Satan has another strategy for America. It is not stamping it out; it is flooding the market with something that is legal. In that way, you and I will take it for granted and read it as little as someone who does not own a copy. However, the word of God has been preserved.

I love the story of Voltaire, who was an atheist. He once bragged, "You have seen what a little fellow by the name of Paul has done for Christianity, now I will show you what a Frenchmen will do to destroy Christianity." Yet, to this very day, the Geneva Bible Printing Society has as its headquarters, Voltaire's own home! They print Bibles in his former living room. God preserves His word.

Transformed lives

The Bible is the only book that can turn a sinner into a saint.

This past week, someone brought a book into the office of stories about men and poems they had written. I began paging through the book and found a story I remembered reading before. It was a story about John Newton.

John Newton was born in London in 1725. His father was a sea captain and his mother was a devout believer. His mother had an illness that she knew would soon take her life, so she invested every spare moment teaching her young son God's word. When John was seven, she did in fact, die, and he became a cabin boy aboard a sailing vessel.

John Newton began a life of terrible sin that would one day see him captain of a slave ship. He was a drunken sinner, and in fact, his crew considered him nothing more than an animal. That was exemplified on one occasion when John Newton fell overboard. His crew did not even let down a boat to rescue him, but instead, took a whaling harpoon and threw it at him. It caught him in the hip and they pulled him back on board as they would a large fish.

John Newton limped the rest of the days of his life, but the grace of God gripped his heart. He, one day, came to Christ, remembering the words of his mother from Ephesians 2:8a,

For by grace you have been saved through faith . . .

8

As an act of appreciation and gratitude to his Lord, he would write the words that we sing so often,

Amazing grace! How sweet the sound,

That saved a wretch like me;

I once was lost, but now I'm found,

Was blind, but now I see.

One verse is no longer in our hymn books, but was in the original poem written by John Newton. I like it because it has a direct relation to the transforming power of God's word. It says,

The Lord has promised good to me,

His word my hope secures;

He willed my shield and portion be,

As long as life endures.

The Bible can turn a sinner into a saint. The greatest illustration of that is not John Newton, but you. Is God's word part of your life?

Archeological proof

Now, this is not a proof to a nonbeliever, but it is an assurance to those who already believe. The reason for that is because there is only one way that you will ever come to the point where you believe that the Bible is God's book, and that is by faith. But once you have that faith, then logic can prevail and you can see all the reasons that men without faith missed.

I could preach on this archeological proof for a long time, but I will give just a couple of illustrations.

The first illustration is the city of Pithom that was recently uncovered. It was built by Rameses II, or actually by the Hebrew slaves during the reign of Rameses II. This was a period in their captivity known as hard labor. When this city was uncovered, it was discovered that the homes were made of sun baked bricks – some of which had straw in them, while some did not. In other words, this find displayed exactly what we find described in the book of Exodus, chapter 5, when the Hebrew slaves were commanded to make bricks without straw.

The Old Testament scriptures also speak of another city that we call Petra. This city was one that many liberals and infidels had long mocked. The critics scoffed and asked, "Where is your city Petra that the Bible mentions?" Then one day, archeologists discovered a city built into a mountain of stone, and it was as if gigantic mountains watched over it, as stone guards. It was a city built into solid rock, just as the Bible declared. When it was finally discovered, the archaeologists found within that stone tomb, a city with homes, theaters, temples, places of business, and a main street six miles long.

There is no need to be afraid of the archaeologist's spade. They have done nothing but substantiate the words of scripture and declare that the Bible is entirely true.

Let me give a second reason that we study God's word in its entirety – not only because it is entirely true, but because it is entirely profitable.

The Bible is the primary source for equipping the believer

Turn to II Timothy 3. Let us look at several passages that declare this to every believer. In verses 14 through 17, we will notice four things that the word does that make it profitable to the believer.

Look at II Timothy 3:14, 15. Paul writes to Timothy, his son in the faith,

> *You, however, continue in the things you have learned and become convinced of, knowing from whom you have learned them, and that from childhood you have known the sacred writings which are able to give you the wisdom that leads to salvation through faith which is in Christ Jesus.*

Then, Paul declares to him a truth about the word, in verse 16a.

> *All scripture is inspired by God . . .*

The word "inspiration" means, "the breath of God". So this literally means that God breathed through the author or the human instrument. It was the wind or breath of God. In fact, we find this same original word used in the book of Acts, when it talks about the wind blowing into the sails of a vessel. It is that same thought of the wind or the breath of God blowing through the author; the human instrument. It is God directing him to write exactly what we find here. All scripture then, is breathed by God.

Four things scripture is profitable for

Continue to II Timothy 3:16b,

. . . and profitable for teaching, for reproof, for correction, for training in righteousness;

All scripture is also profitable for four things. Let us briefly look at them.

1. Teaching or doctrine

Doctrine is what you believe. Doctrine tells you how to think..

I have frequently heard, and believed until recent years that we know enough about the Bible, we just do not apply enough of the Bible. I now reject that statement because I believe there is a famine in the land as to what the Bible teaches. We do not know enough about the Bible. And the Bible is profitable for doctrinal function; for truth.

2. Reproof or rebuke

This tells you where you are wrong. Doctrine tells you what to think or how to believe; reproof tells you where you are wrong.

3. Correction

This tells you what is right.

4. Training in righteousness

This tells you how to do what is right.

Move on to verse 17.

so that the man of God may be adequate, equipped for every good work.

I think the main part of this scripture is that the Bible is the primary source for equipping the believer. Without it you stand naked against the attack of the evil one in the world. It is this Bible that will equip you. It is profitable.

The Bible is the primary assurance for a credible testimony

Now turn to II Timothy, chapter 2. This gives us another thought about the profitability of the word of God. Let us read verse 15.

Be diligent to present yourself approved to God as a workman who does not need to be ashamed, accurately handling [or rightly dividing] the word of truth.

I heard one man say that this verse is the "bottom line" of Christianity. The bottom line is found in two questions, which are:

- Am I pleasing to Jesus Christ? We are to be a workman who is pleasing to God.

- Is my life measuring up to the standard of scripture? We are to be studying God's word in such a way that we are not ashamed. In fact, the literal translation of verse 15 could be, "a workman whose work is never a disgrace". That is the idea.

I think the main idea in this passage is that with the word as the primary assurance, there will be creditability in your testimony. Without the study of scripture, your walk will never match up, as they say, to your talk.

I read a poem that says the gospel is written a chapter a day by the deeds that you do and the words that you say. Men read what you say whether faithless or true. What is the gospel according to you?

The only way the gospel will have creditability is if we are studying this book, the Bible.

The Bible is the primary guarantee for spiritual maturity

Turn to Hebrews, chapter 5. Here we are told that the Bible is the primary guarantee to spiritual maturity.

Look at verse 11.

Concerning him we have much to say, and it is hard to explain, since you have become dull of hearing.

There was a problem with this church – a hearing problem. It was a spiritual hearing problem. They had to have things repeated over and over again. And as a result, he compares them to a child.

Read on to Hebrews 5:12-14.

For though by this time you ought to be teachers, you have need again for someone to teach you the elementary principles of the oracles of God, and you have come to need milk and not solid food. For everyone who partakes only of milk is not accustomed to the word of righteousness, for he is an infant. But solid food is for the mature, . . .

(Who are the mature?),

. . . who because of practice have their senses trained to discern good and evil.

This is saying that spiritual maturity is not simply learning about this book, but it is practicing this book. The spiritually mature individual is one who begins to live what he has learned. I think the only way we can have the guarantee that we will in fact, live what is learned, which is spiritual maturity, comes from this book, the Bible.

The Bible is the primary method for spiritual growth

Let me add one other passage that continues this same thought and gives the main idea that the Bible is the primary method for spiritual growth. Turn to I Peter 2.

I Peter 2:1, 2 says,

Therefore, putting aside all malice and all deceit and hypocrisy and envy and all slander, like newborn babies, long for the pure milk of the word, so that by it you may grow in respect to salvation,

Why does God want you and I to study the Bible? So that we can become smarter? Absolutely not. He wants us to study the Bible so that we can become transformed; so that we may grow up.

The implication in these verses is that it is possible to grow old in the Lord, without growing up in the Lord. I fear that there are many believers who are five, ten, fifteen, and twenty years old in the Lord, but are still in the nursery.

My friends, without this book, we stay in the crib; without understanding the words of scripture, we become or remain an infant. Someone always has to come along and feed or dress us. Why? Because we have long refused to allow this book to be part of our lives and to transform and renew our minds.

So, the Bible is the primary method for spiritual growth.

I would suggest to you not to pray anymore that God will help you grow, but to pray that God will give you diligence to study the word. When you do, you will grow.

Why do we study the Bible? Because the Bible is entirely true and because the Bible is entirely profitable.

Exposition

Turn to the first chapter of Genesis. Today, we are going to take a few moments to introduce the first verse and then, in our next discussion, we will take a more detailed survey of the six days of creation.

Genesis 1:1 stands by itself. It should – it is a foundational verse. Look at that verse.

In the beginning God created the heavens and the earth.

Let us dissect these words for the sake of study. We will look at the words individually and then, put them together into one unit.

In the beginning

- The first words are, "In the beginning . . .". This could be translated literally as, "In the beginning of things". In other words, before there was anything other than God – this is when He began.

Now I have got to admit to you, ladies and gentlemen, in my study, I so often scratch my head. It would have seemed so much better if God had written one hundred words instead of the ten that we have in our English translation. There are seven words in the original Hebrew language. We might think, "Lord, it would have been so much easier if You had just written a book on verse 1 and given us all of the details." But He did not do that. Perhaps that is what the writer of Hebrews meant when he said in Hebrews 11:3a,

By faith we understand that the worlds were prepared by the word of God . . .

Whether there are ten words or a thousand, believing it is still a matter of faith. Questions will never be completely answered and understood until we get to heaven and then, it will take all of eternity before we truly comprehend.

God

- The next word is, "In the beginning God . . .". The original Hebrew word is the word "Elohim," which is a beautiful, powerful name of God.

The word "Elohim" means, "God of Power". This name will appear many times in the Old Testament. It is rightly used in this verse because this act of miraculously creating the worlds is an act of great power. So, when the writer seeks to express who this individual is; when God would express Himself through the writer, He chooses the name "Elohim," or "the God of Power". This name always pulls a response from us of trust and awe.

As I read, "In the beginning God . . .", and read it and read it, it became clear to me again that things are left out. There is no proof for the existence of God in Genesis, chapter 1, verse 1. There is no argument, and in fact, the Bible is silent when it comes to arguing the proof of existence.

Why? I think we are given a clue as to why in the only verse that even remotely mentions this. Look at Psalm 14:1,

The fool has said in his heart, "There is no God."

In other words, it is not going to be discussed because it is the fool who does not believe that there is a God.

Genesis 1:1, it is a simple statement, not a deduction; it is a declaration, not an explanation; it is revelation. He is simply saying, "In the beginning God . . .". We can take it or leave it; believe it or not. This is a fundamental statement that needs no proof.

When we study the book of Romans, we will discover in chapter 1 that every man and every woman that has ever lived is without an excuse. Why? Because written on the heart of every human being is the fact that there is a God. In fact, if you go to some remote part of Africa and find some tribe in a jungle that has never before been discovered, guess what you would find them doing? Worshiping something. A missionary does not go to the field to tell people there is a God, he goes to the field to tell them how to get to the true God.

So, He merely states, "In the beginning God . . .".

Created

- Notice the next word, "In the beginning God created . . .". The word in Hebrew is "bara," which means, "created out of nothing".

This is not a Hebrew word that means to form or to fashion, but one that means, "to create out of nothing". God did not form something that already existed; He did not pattern after something already in existence, God created out of nothing, planet earth and the heavens.

The heavens and the earth

- The verse then says, "In the beginning God created the heavens and the earth." "The heavens" could be translated as "space," and "the earth" as a little reference to "this planet" or to "matter".

So, in the first verse of Genesis, chapter 1, we find that God created space, matter, and time. "In the beginning" – time; "God created the heavens" – space; "and the earth" – matter.

No scientist could ever improve on Genesis 1:1. If they by faith believe it, then they have the logical answer of the creation of everything that ever has been.

Oh, I know that scientists scrap for theories, and that even today, there is the theory of evolution. In fact, I read of one scientist who said that in the space of twenty or thirty years, that particular theory will be replaced by another.

Theories have always existed. The theory of evolution just happens to be one for our generation; one for our time. Theories of the origins of the earth and of space have changed through time because after thorough investigation, they have been shown to be untrue.

An unbeliever might suggest that this view of Genesis 1:1, is narrow and there is no room for anything other than that God created the heavens and earth. I would say, "Yes, it is narrow. All truth is narrow. What would you think of a mathematician who said, 'I am no

16

good at mathematics for I am liberal and open minded and 2 + 2 could equal 3.999.'?"

You would think they were foolish, for 2 + 2 will always equal 4. Never did a math teacher, including mine, give any credit for any answer that was only close to the correct one. It had to be dead on.

The truth of the scripture is very narrow, my friends. In the days of Noah, there was salvation and there was only one way. You were either in the ark or you were out of the ark. In the days of Moseś, deliverance came only one way. You either had the blood on the door post or you did not have the blood on the door post. Today, the scripture tells us that if you believe in the Son of God, you will have eternal life; if you do not, you will have the wrath of God upon you. It is that narrow; it is that simple; it is that plain.

May I suggest to you that this verse, Genesis 1:1, provides a foundation upon which every other verse in the Bible rests. If you can believe, ladies and gentlemen, the first ten words of scripture,

In the beginning God created the heavens and the earth.

. . . then you will have no problem believing eleven other words in II Corinthians 5:17a,

Therefore if anyone is in Christ, he is a new creature . . .

If you can believe,

In the beginning God created the heavens and the earth.

. . then you can believe John 3:16 that,

For God so loved the world, that He gave His only begotten Son, that whoever believes in Him shall not perish, but have eternal life.

If you by faith can believe these first ten words, then you can believe all of scripture.

Application

Let me apply this foundation of study in three ways.

1. Preaching/teaching the Bible is not voluntary, it is imperative.

Let me suggest to you, ladies and gentlemen, that we are not to preach *about* the Bible. We live in a generation that has literally sapped the vitality out of the Christian world because pulpits are filled with men who preach about the Bible.

One of the things that I fear, is preaching something other than the very words of scripture. I had a professor in college who told us on one occasion, that his greatest fear was preaching error.

One of the questions I believe you should ask yourself as a Sunday school teacher, or as a preacher, or as a teacher is, "Did I preach/teach the word?"

Paul told Timothy, in II Timothy 4:1, 2 to preach the word – and there is an exclamation point after that in the original text. It is imperative.

2. Studying the Bible is not optional, it is essential.

If it is the only method for spiritual growth, it is the only guarantee for spiritual credibility. If it is the only promise or hope of spiritual maturity, this is all we have. The question is not "Should I study it?" but "How can I afford not to?"

3. Obeying the Bible is not suggested, it is demanded

A recent archeological find in the biblical city of Heshbon (Joshua 21:39), presents an ironic twist – sixty-two pounds of cut up silver jewelry was discovered stored in five earthen jars. Even more significant is that this discovery was not found in some mount in the middle of nowhere, but eighteen inches under the earthen floor of a home that had been lived in by individuals over the past three centuries. There were people who had these valuable things within their grasp. You can almost imagine the reaction of someone who discovered that after they had moved. They would probably say something like, "Oh, if I had only known! I would have dug down and gotten it for myself."

My friends, I submit to you that we have in front of us, a treasure house filled with precious gems. I would encourage you to bring your Bible with you when you come to church on Sunday. And I would suggest that we are far more willing to do that than we are to walk across the living room floor and pick it up during the week. My friend did you dust your Bible off when you came to church this morning? Is the word at work in your life? Is this Book having a transforming effect on your daily existence?

The challenging thing is that when I get out of sorts; when my life gets out of balance, it is directly traceable to the fact that I either do not know what the word says, or I am not obeying what I know that the word says.

The Book of Beginnings

Genesis 1:1

Digging Deeper :

II Timothy 3: 16a *All scripture is inspired by God and profitable for teaching, for reproof, for correction, for training in righteousness;*

Notice the word "All", in the above verse. God does not tell us that "Some" of the Bible is profitable. He does not say, "choose the part you can live by, throw out the rest, and that part is profitable." No, He says, "All."

God has given us His Word, both Old Testament and New Testament. He has reveled His Will to us through His Word. God has told us what He wants us to know. We are forbidden to add to it or subtract from it.

1) How was scripture inspired and what profit can come from it?

_____

_____

_____

_____

II Timothy 3:17 *so that the man of God may be adequate, equipped for every good work.*

Why should we study the Bible? God is revealed to us through the Bible. By studying all of Scripture, we come to know the character, attributes, and nature of God. We were created to worship and glorify God. To glorify God means to truly understand who He is. How could we hope to glorify God if we do not know what God wants us to know about Him?

At the same time, we need to be very careful to study the **true** Word of God found in the Old and New Testaments. One of Satan's schemes is to proliferate God's word throughout the world, slightly changed, slightly wrong, slightly contradictory. When we see these false messages, we become confused. How can we avoid this confusion? Read God's **true** Word. Study God's **true** Word. Know God's **true** Word. When the false words come, you will be adequately equipped to glorify God.

2) Why do we need to be equipped?

_____

_____

_____

_____

Genesis 1:1 *In the beginning God created the heavens and the earth.*

What a start to a book.! *In the beginning **God**...* Aren't we missing something? Shouldn't there be a book or two explaining who this God is?

3) Why doesn't the Bible begin with a defense of God's existence?

_____

_____

_____

_____

It is inherent in every human to know that a creator exists. We are searching for something or someone to worship. We know that some powerful being exists. It has been said that even Satan knows that God exists. Satan is not spending his time denying the existence of God. He is trying to show us that his way is better than

21

God's way. Thus, the Bible does not need to start with a defense of God's existence. The Bible will focus on showing us God's **true** way. This is where we need to focus. All of creation knows that God exists.

So, we believe that God exists, but what kind of God? Somewhat powerful?...A little knowledgeable?...*God created the heavens and the earth.* Really **focus** on that phrase...***God created the heavens and the earth....***If God could create the heavens and the earth, is there anything that this Creator can not do? If He can do this, then He must also be able to control everything He created. This Creator has given His creation a standard to live by, shown to us through the Bible. And this same Creator will one day judge his creation.

John 3:16 *For God so loved the world, that He gave His only begotten Son, that whoever believes in Him shall not perish, but have eternal life.*

If you believe in a God that is the creator of the universe, then how hard is it be to believe in a God that would send His Son to earth to provide a way for his creation to live with Him eternally?

4) How is Genesis 1:1 foundational for the rest of the bible?

_____

_____

_____

_____

_____

Take It To Heart :

Recently, a young lady was baptized in our church. The pastor asked her to share a testimony with the congregation. She shared that her father had a significant effect on her coming to know the Lord. She said that daily she would see her father reading his Bible.

Did you "dust off" your bible when you went to church last?

How can we know the Lord and His plan for us without reading His instructions? He has given us a model to live our lives by, we just need to read and study the model. Next we need to implement the model in our lives. It is not enough just to read the Bible. Bible study is not just to be an information gathering exercise. We must live the truths of the Bible. We must use what we learn!

How is the word at work in your life?

Think of your home. Name 5 ways you are modeling God's instructions in your home. (Family, TV, quiet time, etc…)

_____

_____

_____

_____

_____

Is the truth of God's word a part of your daily existence?
How can you make it so?

And God Said . . .

Genesis 1:1-23

Introduction

It is against the first few chapters of Genesis that Satan has launched his fiercest attack. And rightly so, because, as I suggested in our last discussion, if a person can believe the first two chapters of Genesis, he can believe all of scripture.

If a person can believe by faith that God created the heavens and the earth, as we are told in the first chapter of Genesis, then he can, by faith, believe in the last few chapters of Revelation. Here we are told that God will create a new heaven and a new earth. Genesis provides the basis for such faith.

May I remind you, ladies and gentlemen, that if Genesis, chapter 1, is wrong, then Jesus, who confirmed this record, and the prophets, who declared this record, and the apostles, who continued to teach this record are all pathological liars. And as well, our faith has become mere delusion.

All that we believe, men and women, hangs in the balance of Genesis, chapters 1 and 2. And Satan knows that full well. I think that is why he has kept up his attack using mirages and theories against these first two chapters in the beginning of the Bible.

Let me read a few theories. And, by the way, I want you to understand that theories are not new – they have been around as long as man, as you will soon learn.

In 1808, there were catalogued at least eighty theories of man's origin. There were theories that we came from seaweed; theories that we come from apes; and more recently, the theory propounded by a scientist that we evolved from garbage left on this earth by some prehistoric intelligence. Perhaps that is why my kids always mess up their rooms – they inherited that from the garbage dump they evolved from!

After nearly two hundred years, scientists are now openly admitting their frustration. One Swedish botanist by the name of Dr. Herbert Nilsson, who is an evolutionist and not a believer, wrote these words,

My attempts to demonstrate evolution by experiment carried on for more than forty years have completely failed. It may be firmly maintained that it is not possible to find nor construct new classes (species). Deficiencies are real. They will never be filled. The idea of an evolution rests on pure belief.

You are lead to believe that this theory is based on fact and that Christian beliefs are based on mere faith, but both are based on faith.

The Texas Board of Education recently wrote an article, and I will quote David Hogy who said the following,

Teachers of undergraduate students; that is, junior and senior high, elementary and on up through college. Teachers are urged to stop brainwashing their students. You have legal and grave responsibility, teachers, to be truthful and honest and to fulfill your responsibility by presenting students with the facts that evolution is unproven. It is impossible that the universal natural laws of dynamics reversed themselves to accommodate the theory of evolution.

Now, in case your memory of science is like mine, let me remind you of something that you may have learned and I was supposed to have learned. I learned it best this past week by review. One of the laws basically states that things go from good to bad. In other words, things begin with intelligence and become dumb; things begin strong and become weak. For example, look at a building; look at an oil painting; look at the human body. The evolutionist would declare that those laws were reversed so that some amoeba floating in some murky puddle decided to become more intelligent until it finally reached its peak of intelligence, and then the laws began digressing. No one would believe that. As if some amoeba wanted to become more intelligent.

An article in *Life* magazine concerning the origin of life said that at some indeterminate point – some say two billion years ago, while others say a billion and a half (they play with millions of years like we play with our budget!), something took form that science cannot specify. All that can be said is that through some agency, certain molecules acquired the ability to duplicate themselves.

Imagine that, a giant molecule one day said, "Hey, I think I'll make another one of me."

Poof! There was another molecule.

That is foolish. That is like putting a rooster in a hen house all by himself and saying, "Lets wait a million years and we will get some eggs. We just need to wait and be patient."

No one would believe that.

Let me read a recent article from UCLA at Berkeley that would fit the statement that I read by one scientist who said, "The data we have today fits the creation model better than the evolutionary model."

The article said,

Biochemists have concluded by their study of mitochondria DNA that if family trees were charted indefinitely backward, they would ultimately converge on a small group of ancients who were ancestors of us all.

In other words, if we went back far enough, we would go back to one family. Boy, that is unique, isn't it?

The article continued to say that they think a single female is an ancestor of everyone on earth today. Guess what they have nicknamed her? Eve.

Man searches for his origins; the world wants a beginning, and they search. What we have, ladies and gentlemen, in Genesis, chapter 1, is the beginning.

Three Reasons for the Creation Account

Now, as we approach this study, we should at least stop for a moment to answer three questions as to why God gave the creation account. Let me give three reasons for the creation account.

1. To encourage Israel's faith

This God, the God who claims to be their creator, is the same God who lead them into the promised land. And He told them to follow Him and they would conquer it. He had better be a powerful God. Moses declares His phenomenal omnipotence. God is powerful – and it bolsters their faith.

2. To refute the myths about origins

As I said, theories are not new. We have the Babylonian creation aspects that have come down through time. We can read that in the time of the Israelites, there were also evolutionary theories. There were theories that men were fallen gods; that somehow God procreated and came up with humanity. There were the myths then, and God wanted to set the record straight. So, He refutes all the myths.

3. To paint a portrait of God's character

Genesis, chapter 1, reveals God's sovereignty, His power, His relationship to men and the world. In fact, Genesis 1, refers to God no less than thirty-two times in one chapter.

The Length of Days in the Creation Account

Now, as we study this chapter, let us divide it into two sections. We will study:

- The length of the days of the creation account;
- The activity found in each day of the creation account.

We will begin with the length of the days of the creation account. In Genesis 1, does the length of a day refer to a literal twenty-four hour solar day? In all of these events, do the days follow one after the other as day follows night and night follows day?

The theorist would suggest that these are not to be taken literally and that the word "day" represents age. So, a day could mean a million years or perhaps, a billion years, meaning a day does not refer to twenty-four hours.

There are many in churches, by the way, who preach that it is possible to have one foot in Genesis and one foot in evolution. It is called "theistic evolution". This is the belief that God began and then, over a process of millions of years things would evolve.

So, it is very important that we understand whether the creation account "day" means a twenty-four hour day or millions of years for each day, which would allow evolution of all that is recorded in Genesis, chapter 1.

Three proofs for a literal interpretation

Let me give you three reasons why I believe this is literally twenty-four hour days. I might also add, these are days without any gaps.

1. Each day has an evening and a morning

Notice this, as you read through Genesis 1. Look at verse 5b.

... And there was evening and there was morning, one day.

Look at verse 8b.

... And there was evening and there was morning, a second day.

This is common Hebrew phraseology for a literal solar day. It is even foolish that we would take the time to declare such obvious truth.

Men and women, as we study the Bible, it is clear that God wrote what He meant. If He had not written what He meant, how would we ever know what He meant? So, it is as simple as reading the account for yourself.

2. Each day is accompanied by a number

Notice, as we read the phrase "there was evening and there was morning," that it was accompanied by a number of the day; such as, "a second day." Any time and every time we read the word "day," or "yom" in the Hebrew, it is accompanied by a numerical adjective. It always refers to a literal day – never figurative.

3. God summarizes all the acts of creation

Look at two additional passages in Genesis 2:1, 2a.

Thus the heavens and the earth were completed, and all their hosts. By the seventh day God completed His work which He had done, ...

Notice the way God summarizes all the acts of creation. Some would say that there is a gap between chapters 1 and 2. I do not believe that. Genesis 2:1 says that the heavens and the earth were completed and all their hosts – that is the activity of Genesis 1:1 – and then, by the seventh day, God completed His work.

Look at Exodus, chapter 20, which contains the Ten Commandments. You probably did not realize they are proof of creation as well. Look at Exodus 20:9-11a.

Six days you shall labor and do all your work, but the seventh day is a Sabbath of the Lord your God; in it you shall not do any work, you or your son or your daughter, your male or your female servant or your cattle or your sojourner who stays with you. For in six days the Lord made the heavens and the earth, the sea and all that is in them, and rested on the seventh day; ...

This is conclusive and comprehensive. God did everything that He did in six literal days, and then, He rested on the seventh. It is as clear as scripture.

The Activity of Each Day in the Creation Account

Now let us look at the activity of each day in the creation account.

Day One (Genesis 1:1-5)

In the beginning God created the heavens and the earth. The earth was formless and void, and darkness was over the surface of the deep, and the spirit of God was moving over the surface of the waters. Then God said, "Let there be light"; and there was light. God saw that the light was good; and God separated the light from the darkness. God called the light day, and the darkness He called night. And there was evening and there was morning, one day.

Let me give three things that occurred on the first day.

- God created light. This was not bodies that would give off light or reflect light, but simply light.
- God divided light from darkness. He drew the boundaries and divided light from darkness.
- God named the light day and the darkness night.

I could not help but notice, as I read this chapter, that God not only created objects, things, creatures, and later, mankind, but He also created a vocabulary. The first chapter of Genesis gives us the origin of many words that people use all of the time, whether they believe in creation or not. For example, we might say, "Boy, it is a beautiful day today." or "Tomorrow is Monday morning." or "Is it dark yet?" or "What are we having for supper this evening?" In this chapter, words were created; such as: light, darkness, day, evening, morning, water, heavens, the dry lands, sea, earth, vegetation, seeds, trees, plants, fruits, cattle. Everyone in this world borrows heavily from the Genesis account. In fact, if all of the words from the first few chapters of Genesis were taken out of your vocabulary, you would be linguistically stunted.

Day Two (Genesis 1:6-8)

Then God said, "Let there be an expanse in the midst of the waters, and let it separate the waters from the waters. God made the expanse, and separated the waters which were below the expanse from the waters which were above the expanse; and it was so. God called the expanse heaven. And there was evening and there was morning, a second day.

Now God will create the firmament and He does that by dividing water. So far, all we have is earth covered by water.

This is not the appearance of dry land – that will happen a little later – and there is then a creation of the firmament whereby God creates heaven. This is the first heaven; this is where the birds fly and the clouds float by; this is the expanse. So, there is the water below covering the surface of the earth, the heaven, and then, He creates a body of water above, according to the text, which is a vaporous canopy.

This allowed for two things; two hidden things that God created as well.

- God created the conditions for paradise.

The conditions God created were paradise. The canopy of water above kept all the harmful rays of the sun away. In fact, there is only warmth. Because of this greenhouse effect, the world is a tropical region and the temperatures are constant and warm. There is no need for clothing, and in fact, Adam and Eve did not wear any. After the fall, they would wear clothing not because of the temperatures, but because of lost innocence. This is a world wide fertile region where the grasses would grow and the fruit trees would flourish. It was paradise.

It will one day be paradise again. There will be an absence of seasons and it will be constantly warm. That will mean a whole lot more to us when our winter season begins!

- God not only created the conditions for paradise, but He also created the potential for judgment.

When man's rebellion reached its horrible climax, God told Noah to build an ark. Why? Because He was going to flood the earth. This is, of course, after the dry land appeared and mankind is flourishing.

Now, where is God going to get the water to flood the earth? I read this past week, if all of the clouds surrounding this globe were to drop all of the water they carried, and if that water spread evenly around this globe, it would only be as deep as about one and a half inches. Now where is God going to get enough water so that it covers the face of the earth to in fact, fifteen cubits above the highest mountain? That is a few gallons of water!

In the Genesis account given in chapter 7, we are told that God nudges the vapor above, collapsing it, and water then deluges planet earth.

This thing that was created by God to allow fertile paradise living will now be that with which He judges planet earth. So He created this planet with the ability to produce and provide enjoyment, but also to destroy and to kill.

There is also another judgment coming. Turn to II Peter 3. I want you to notice a pattern that God established. II Peter 3:6, tells us that the first judgment was water. Then verse 7 will tell us that the second judgment will be by fire. Look at II Peter 3:3-7.

Know this first of all, that in the last days mockers will come with their mocking, following after their own lusts, and saying, "Where is the promise of His coming? For ever since the fathers fell asleep, all continues just it was from the beginning of creation." For when they maintain this, it escapes their notice that by the word of God the heavens existed long ago and the earth was formed out of water and by water, through which the world at that time was destroyed, being flooded with water.

(Notice God used the water He had created to destroy the world.) Following in verse 7,

But by His word the present heavens and earth are being reserved for fire, kept for the day of judgment and destruction of ungodly men.

How is God going to destroy the present heaven and earth? I think He is going to nudge what He has already created and fire will burn earth to a cinder.

Now, I am considerably out of my field when I deal with scientific or mathematical facts. I did not do well in math and when I got to college, they looked at my records and said, "You need to repeat math."

So, they put me in a college course that we labeled as being for all of the "bone heads". I studied that math and barely squeaked out of there. However, I have been reminded this past week, while studying several things that will explain why I believe God will destroy the world by fire.

Seventy four percent of the earth is covered with water. Now water is the liquid form of H_2O, and I can remember that. That would be one atom of oxygen and two atoms of hydrogen. Now, what if Christ were to remove His sustaining hand? We know from Colossians 1:17,

He [Christ] is before all things, and in Him all things hold together.

He holds all things together and that includes molecules and atoms. What if God took away His hand? And what if that simple molecule of water was split so that the hydrogen was split from the oxygen? All waters, all seventy four percent that covers the face of this earth and exists as water vapor in the air would instantly turn to flammable gas. Then, it would only take one little spark somewhere on planet earth and the fire ball would destroy this planet inside and out.

Do you know what I think? I think there is a pattern here. God has created this earth with the ability to provide for life, but He has also preserved it for judgment because of sin.

Day Three (Genesis 1:9-13)

> *Then God said, "Let the waters below the heavens be gathered into one place, and let the dry land appear"; and it was so. God called the dry land earth, and the gathering of the waters He called seas; and God saw that is was good. Then God said, "Let the earth sprout vegetation, plants yielding seed, and fruit trees bearing fruit after their kind, with seed in them, on the earth"; and it was so. And the earth brought forth vegetation, plants yielding seed after their kind, and trees bearing fruit, with seed in them, after their kind; and God saw that it was good. There was evening and there was morning, a third day.*

Notice there is no mention of oceans. Perhaps that is a remnant of the flood.

There are two key phrases in this text that I want you to note.

- The first key phrase is "bearing fruit".

I think He is obviously saying that the trees were created in their mature state. When God created anything on planet earth, He created it in its already mature state. When He created man and woman, He created them as mature adults. There was no little baby Adam or little baby Eve – they were adults. When God created or spoke into existence a fruit tree, it was already bearing fruit. This is in the present tense.

I think it is important to note that when God created this planet, it was in a mature state. So, there was an apple tree bearing apples, and there was an orange tree bearing oranges, and there was a peach tree bearing peaches, and there was a money tree . . . just seeing if you are awake and with me! I think that was the tree that God told Eve to stay away from myself, but I could be wrong . . . or at least in trouble!

- The second key phrase is "after their kind".

The word "kind" is the word "phylum," which means, " a direct line of descent within a group". Why is this important? Because He is telling us that a peach tree will always bear peaches, a monkey will always bear monkeys. There is no such thing as a half beast, half man. God created this universe to reproduce "after their kind".

Day Four (Genesis 1:14-19)

> *Then God said, "Let there be lights in the expanse of the heavens to separate the day from the night, and let them be for signs, and for seasons and for days and years; and let them be for lights in the expanse of the heavens to give light on the earth"; and it was so. God made the two great lights, the greater light to govern the day, and the lesser light to govern the night; He made the stars also. aGod placed them in the expanse of the heavens to give light on the earth, and to govern the day and the night, and to separate the light from the darkness; and God saw that it was good. And there was evening and there was morning,, a fourth day.*

So, God creates the sun, the moon, and the stars, and they were also created in their mature state. When He created the stars, their reflecting light was already reaching earth.

The evolutionist would declare earth to be an old earth. They would say, "You see that star out there? We know that to be three million light years away, so it would take three million light years for its rays to reach to planet earth."

However, if God created everything in its mature state, then when He created the star, He also created the trail of lights so that it was immediately reaching planet earth. So, we could still have, in effect, a young earth.

I think there are reasons other than just to give light that God created the lights. Let me give two reasons.

- The first reason is that the lights give constant illustrations to us.

In the word, Jesus Christ is referred to as the Light of the world. Christians are also lights.

Look at a fascinating passage of scripture in Philippians 2:14, 15. Paul is writing to the church at Philippi and says of the believer,

> *Do all things without grumbling or disputing; so that you will prove yourselves to be blameless and innocent, children of God above reproach in the midst of a crooked and perverse generation, among whom you appear as lights in the world,*

This literally could be translated as reflected lights.

- The second reason is that we reflect the light of the Son.

I think the stars and the moon of heaven remind us that we reflect the light of Jesus Christ.

I also think the created lights are constant reminders of the coming paradise. Revelation, chapters 21 and 22, tells us that one day, we will not have need of the sun or of the moon or of the stars to shine because the light of God's glory and presence will pervade heaven and the new earth. Every time we look up, we can think that one day they will be unnecessary, because it will be the light of God that will light our world.

Day Five (Genesis 1:20-23)

We will stop after these verses as we will only deal with the first five days in today's discussion.

Then God said, "Let the waters team with swarms of living creatures, and let birds fly above the earth in the open expanse of the heavens." God created the great sea monsters and every living creature that moves, with which the waters swarmed after their kind, and every winged bird after its kind; and God saw that it was good. God blessed them, saying, "Be fruitful and multiply, and fill the waters in the seas, and let birds multiply on the earth." There was evening and there was morning, a fifth day.

These verses provide fantastic illustrations for the believer as well. Look at the bird, which illustrates that God cares for us, as Matthew, chapter 6, tells us. Solomon tells us in the Proverbs to go to the animal kingdom and learn wisdom by their activity.

However, I think we are to learn something else from the animal kingdom. Look at Job 12:7-10. Man speculates about origins; man searches for the beginnings, but Job says,

But now ask the beasts, and let them teach you; and the birds of the heavens, and let them tell you. Or speak to the earth, and let it teach you; and let the fish of the sea declare to you. Who among all these does not know that the hand of the Lord has done this. In whose hand is the life of every living thing, and the breath of all mankind?

That is really clear, isn't it? If the fish could speak, they would tell you that we were created by the hand of God. If a bird could speak, he would speak to you of God's hand in creating you. If even the animals know, why is it that man, the one who has been given the ability to logically reason, declares something else. Even the animals know better than that.

Darwin, in fact, admitted the human eye was so complex that he wondered if he should even believe his theory of evolution. He could not even figure out the eye, because it was so complex.

John Wesley, writing of God's display of power in creating the world said, "God created the heavens and the earth and He did not even half try."

I have read that people of old wrote three words above their doorways in Latin, "nice dominus grustra," which translated means, "without God, frustration".

Is it any wonder today that man is frustrated in his attempts to discover his origin, when he is doing it without God? Is it any wonder that men, women, and young people are frustrated in trying to find a fulfilling life? Why? Because they are doing it without God.

When I think of evolution, as chapter 1 of Genesis so comparably combats, I think of the tragedy of what this is teaching the young people of this country with regard to their worth. What kind of value do you have if your ancestor is an amoeba from some murky puddle? What kind of worth do you have if you trace your ancestry far enough back and find your great, great . . . ancestor is an ape? No wonder man is frustrated.

My friend, you learn your value and worth when you discover by faith that you have been created by a loving God who created you in His own image. That is fulfillment.

Application

I will end with only one application as we continue our study of Genesis, chapter 1. The application is, if God is indeed our Creator, He has every right, every ability to be our Savior.

My friends, God is your designer, but He wants to be your redeemer.

And God Said . . .

Digging Deeper :

Genesis 1 shows the origin of the earth and of the universe. God is the creator and He made a perfect creation. The facts of creation seem to be under attack more than any other area of the Bible. Why? If we believe that God is the creator, then we must believe that God is all powerful and has the right to rule over each of us as Lord and Savior of our lives. Satan continually attacks the creation facts by presenting theories devoid of a creator. If Satan can move us to believe that there is no creator, then we cannot believe that there is an all powerful God. Once the sovereignty of God is undermined, then all the scriptures are doubtful. That is Satan's objective, to displace the Truth with his lies.

Through the creation act in Genesis 1, God reveals his character to us. From His sovereignty to His relationship to man, God is named over 30 times in Genesis 1.

1) Take your Bible and find each mention of God in Genesis 1. Group these together by the character of God that is revealed.

_____

_____

_____

_____

_____

_____

_____

_____

The first chapter of Genesis gives us the facts of creation. Contained in these verses we find the timeframe and the order of creation. But how long did it really take? Many scholars look for ways to fit creation into an evolution model. For evolution to take place there must be significant time for things to evolve. Reading Genesis 1 literally, does not allow for significant time to pass. Thus, to many scholars, the "creation day" must mean something else. A million years is needed. Or perhaps 2 million years. There must be time for the ameba to "grow up" to be man. The view of evolution is another attempt to remove or diminish God from the origin of the earth and the universe. Remember, if Satan can diminish God in our eyes, he compromises both the sovereignty of God and our significance as His children.

I believe that the Bible means what it says. God's creation was completed in 6 days and then He rested on the seventh day. Each day is a literal, 24 hour day. As the Bible states, each day has a morning and an evening. The Hebrew writer used the normal phraseology to describe a 24 hour solar day. Look at the order of the creation. On day 3 God created vegetation, but He had not yet created a light in the sky and had not yet created the seasons. This came on day 4. If each day, as some scholars believe were a million years, then how could the vegetation live without the warmth from the sun? Day 4 had to come very soon after day 3...Or as Genesis says, 24 hours after day 3.

2) Why is the length of the "creation day" important? And why do evolutionists "need" a longer day?

_____

_____

_____

_____

_____

_____

3) God created earth in a "mature" state. What does this mean? And why is this important?

_____

_____

_____

_____

_____

_____

Genesis 1:11-12 *Then God said, "Let the earth sprout vegetation: plants yielding seed, and fruit trees on the earth bearing fruit after their kind with seed in them"; and it was so. The earth brought forth vegetation, plants yielding seed after their kind, and trees bearing fruit with seed in them, after their kind; and God saw that it was good.*

4) Explain the meaning of the term in the above verse, "...after their kind..." How does this contradict the evolutionist theory?

_____

_____

_____

_____

_____

Have you ever watched a bird? Notice how they pick at the ground to find food. Notice how they find a puddle of water to drink from and to bath in. They find shelter in trees. Birds are not smart enough to plant seeds for future harvest. Yet God provides for this lowly creature. He provides both food and shelter. Man is created in God's image. God made animals for man's pleasure.

> Matthew 6:26 *Look at the birds of the air, that they do not sow, nor reap nor gather into barns, and yet your heavenly Father feeds them. Are you not worth much more than they?*

5) How can animals teach us how much God cares for us?

_____

_____

_____

Take It To Heart :

Satan would certainly like for us to believe the evolution theories. He teaches it in our schools. He distorts God's own words, confusing their original meanings. In order for Satan to exalt himself, he must work to dispel the truth of God's power. False teaching concerning God's amazing handiwork in the form of evolution is a great place to start.

What is our value or worth if we believe the evolution theory?

We were created in the image of God....Now, what is our worth?

The Climax of Creation

Genesis 2:1-23

Introduction

Genesis, chapter 1, is focused on God's specific acts of creating the universe. The last few verses of chapter 1 and into chapter 2, verses 4-23, focus on God's climactic creative act. The creation man and woman.

It is interesting that, as I studied these passages in Genesis 1 and 2 again, it struck me that the name used for God in chapter 1 is the Hebrew name "Elohim," which is the name that speaks of God's power; His majestic strengths. And, as I mentioned in our last discussion, John Wesley wrote, "God created the heavens and the earth and He did not even half try."

That is so true – for God, with all of His power, brought everything into being and into existence by His word. The name "Elohim" is used for Him in this text, and it refers to His power.

However, when we read the accounts of God creating man and woman, we are introduced to a new name for God– the name "Jehovah". Your English translations will probably, in Genesis 2, add the word "Lord" to God, so we read, "Lord God".

Two meanings of the name "Jehovah"

1. The personal God

Jehovah speaks to God's loving covenant care for mankind. Isn't it interesting that as He moves to the account of His creation of man and woman, His name changes. Now the name is not referring to the majestic powerful God, but the loving God, the personal God. You will see Him directly involved in creating man and woman.

2. The covenant keeping God

This is the name that emphasizes God's covenant with mankind. It is a covenant that is not fragile or self-centered; it is one that will last forever; it is sacrificing. That is the thought used in this passage, because God created man and woman, knowing they would sin; knowing they would fall. God knew man and woman would need a redeemer. The covenant keeping God still brought them into existence, as if to say, "I will provide a redeemer for you."

Now, at the end of Genesis 2, He will bring man and woman together with the same idea. The covenant between man and wife should resemble the same as the covenant of God to man. It is not fragile, it is permanent; it is not self-centered, it is self-sacrificing. We, as man and wife, represent the covenant that Jehovah God has for His creatures. So, there is a name change that means so much.

The triune God created male and female "in Our image"

Now, I want you to notice that there is going to be a change as we read through Genesis 1. You may remember, as we have been studying through Genesis, chapter 1, that it talks about every thing being spoken into existence. Repeatedly – in verses 3, 6, 9, 14, and 20 – it says,

Then God said, "Let there be . . ."

However, in verse 26, notice the difference.

Then God said, "Let Us make man . . ."

It is as if the triune God was calling into a conference the fact that They were about to create man.

We know from the New Testament writings that it was actually Jesus Christ and that the words of Christ formed and created the universe and man. He was the person of this triune God that performed the creative act.

However, it is interesting that He changes the wording and then, notice the next phrase,

Let Us make man in Our image . . .

This is not a physical image, for God is spirit. He is speaking to the fact that man will be created with a mind, with emotions, with a will, with immortality, just like God. Man is made in the image of God.

Ladies and gentlemen, the reason you are able to laugh is because God can laugh. He created you like Himself, with the ability to laugh. The reason you can cry is because God can weep. He created you in His own image, with the ability to weep. The reason that you decide, love, choose to do all that you do is because you are created like your

44

creator God in His image. You are capable of doing the things that He has given you to do that resemble His own character.

Now read verse 27,

God created man in His own image, in the image of God He created him; . . .

(note this and underline it),

. . . _male and female_ He created them.

God created both male and female in His own image. They are both immortal souls. They are not toys; they are not objects, they are immortal beings, both male and female.

Notice also, in this verse, that God strikes a death blow to the unisex idea that there is no difference in males and females. I have been startled at things that I have read that suggest the reason boys act like boys and girls act like girls is because parents condition them culturally when they are little. Parents always give a little boy a hammer – and regret that they did! They give a little girl a doll. And because of this, parents cause them to act the way they do. This verse tells us that God created them male, with all the inherent masculine traits, and female, with all the feminine traits.

It has been a real joy for my wife and I to parent both boys and girls. It is fascinating to notice the differences in our children. The boys act a certain way – they are different and yet, they follow the same pattern – usually destructive! They are so much like little boys. Our girls are on an entirely different wavelength. Even at a young age they begin to reveal the feminine qualities inherent in the female nature; inherited from their mother and on back to their mother Eve.

Seeing the differences in our boys and our girls is fascinating. One of the boys will fall down and my one-year-old daughter will rush over and pat him on the head. You can almost hear her saying, "Can I get you anything – milk, juice? Do you want to borrow my pacifier?" She is such a little mother. In fact, what really worries me is that she is beginning to flirt. We are talking about a one-year-old girl! She looks at me and wrinkles up her nose and bats her eyelids, as if she can get her way by doing that with me. She can. Her mother says that she has me wrapped around her finger. That is not true. I am eating out of the palm of her hand, but I am not wrapped around her finger!

The differences are so obvious, even at very young ages. Why is it that way? Because God designed it that way. He made them, male and female.

This also strikes a death blow to the theory that homosexuality can be a satisfying relationship. If a man could satisfy a man, God would have created another man. But He created a woman.

All of the distinctive characteristics that make man and woman so different are part of God's design. So, do not blur the differences; do not try to blend them together. Exemplify and make much of the differences.

I laughed out loud last week as a man told me an election joke. He said that we really do need a woman for President of the United States because they would not spend billions of dollars on nuclear arms. They would shop around until they found them on sale!

We will talk more about the differences and the way they compliment each other in the weeks ahead.

The Forming of Adam (Genesis 2:1-7)

Now notice in Genesis 2:7, the creation of man.

Then the Lord God formed man of dust from the ground, and breathed into his nostrils the breath of life; . . .

(the immortal soul),

. . . and man became a living being.

Man became a living being, or literally, he became living lives; he would never die. Though the clay carrier of his soul would pass away, his soul would live forever. He is immortal. He will live one day either in hell or in heaven eternally.

The words "dust from the ground" could literally be translated, "a lump of earth". God literally took a lump of earth and from it, formed man.

The word "formed" is the same precious word used by the prophet Jeremiah as he talks about the potter taking a lump of clay and putting it on the potter's wheel and forming a vessel. God took infinite care and the nuances of mankind are from the fingers of God, as He created man.

I read this past week that our bodies are actually made up of the same fifteen or sixteen chemical elements that are found in the earth. That is one of the reasons why the soul departs and we go back to the dust of the ground – we are made up of the same chemical elements. In fact, one man wrote that if you boiled man down to those chemical elements, separated them, and sold them on the market, you would get about $4.50. The next time you and I are prone to be proud, remember the elements in our body are worth a little less than $5.00 on the market.

Now I spent a lot of time reading this past week. Let me give some of the results of a particular book that I read and would encourage you to read. The book is entitled, *Fearfully and Wonderfully Made*. I do not want to take a lot of time reading this to you, but I do not by any means have all of this memorized.

Let me give what I discovered about the human body that is so fascinating. And this is where I want to center our attention today. I want to give us a greater appreciation for the creative act of God in the way that He took the time and care to design us. Let me read a few things about different parts of our bodies.

The body comes equipped with an internal police force of about fifty billion white cells. They attack all of the bacterial forms that invade the body. This is an internal thing that takes place every day.

Inside the human eye, there are one hundred seven million cells. Seven million are cones, each loaded to fire off a message to the brain when a photon of light crosses its path. The other one hundred million cells are called rods. They are capable of distinguishing a thousand shades of color. The human brain will receive millions of reports simultaneously from eye cells. The brain absorbs, sorts, and organizes them all to give you an image of what you are looking at.

The normal ear is astounding. It can detect sound frequencies as faintly as one billionth of a centimeter. The vibration is transmitted into your inner ear by three bones. For instance, when a note is struck on the piano, the piston of bones in your inner ear vibrates two hundred fifty six times a second. The brain sorts and records the vibrations that in turn, produce impulses you perceive as someone is striking middle C.

Genesis 2:1-23

A relatively new study that has exploded in the world of genetics is the study of DNA molecules, the strand chemically coiled in a rope-like fashion inside each cell. Now we are breaking it down or actually getting inside each individual cell; the nucleus of the cell. Each cell has a specific purpose inside the body, but yet each one contains in each DNA all of the instructions for the bodies' one hundred thousand genes. That is, of the DNA inside your body, each one of them has a specific purpose and yet, included in the information each DNA knows is the specific purposes of every DNA in your body. They tell us that the DNA can contain enough instructions to fill six million pages. The DNA is so small that all of the genes in your body could fit into an ice cube. Yet, if the DNA were unwound and joined together end to end, the strand would literally stretch from the earth to the sun and back again four hundred times.

Your bones, though unappreciated at times, are created to withstand enormous wear and tear. A normal person will talk on his poor feet nearly three times around the world in a lifetime. It is interesting to know that no engineer has been able to match the simple human bone. They would love to be able to develop a substance as strong and light and efficient as bone. Imagine, it grows continuously, lubricates itself, requires no shutdown time, and repairs itself when damage occurs.

These are only a few facts. We do not have time to get into the miracle of the skin, the senses of touch and taste, or the way that our hand is created. We are, by the way, the only living creature that has the thumb shaped as it is and able to grasp like it does. In fact, Isaac Newton wrote, "If there was no other evidence than the human thumb, I would believe in the existence of God."

It is interesting that we can make a machine and know, even as the machine is being made and before it is even put to work, that we will have to work out all the "bugs" until it finally works. One engineer was looking at a chart of the anatomy of an individual – at all the nerves, muscles, tendons, and all of the different things that make up the human body – and he was heard to exclaim, "Imagine, when God put it together, it worked the first time!"

Imagine that! There were no "bugs" in God's creation of the human body – before the fall.

The Planting of Eden (Genesis 2:8-17)

Now look at Genesis 2:8, 9. This tells of the planting of the garden of Eden.

The Lord God planted a garden toward the east, in Eden; . . .

(the word "Eden" means "delight" – this was paradise),

. . . and there He placed the man whom He had formed. Out of the ground the Lord caused to grow every tree that is pleasing to the sight and good for food; the tree of life also in the midst of the garden, and the tree of the knowledge of good and evil.

Then, the next few verses will talk about the different rivers, the water, and the location. Some, in fact, think Eden may have been located near the Persian Gulf because of the geographical references to the rivers.

Skip to Genesis 2:15.

Then the Lord God took the man and put him into the garden of Eden, to cultivate it and keep it.

The word "garden" is the Hebrew word "gan," which literally means, "enclosure". This was paradise – in fact, the planet earth was paradise itself, and yet, within paradise, God created an enclosure; it had boundaries. It was fertile; it was the place where man would spend his life managing, ruling, dominating, and enjoying. This was Eden; this was the garden inside of paradise where man and woman were to live.

The importance of two trees

Now we have already read the references to two specific trees. Let me give the importance or the significance of these two trees.

1. The tree of life is the symbol of immortality

This tree is the symbol whereby man and woman could live forever. Now we know that the ability to live forever was directly given from God and yet, He used the tree as the symbol of that. Eating of that fruit would be the means, the method, the vehicle through which we would live forever.

2. The tree of the knowledge of good and evil is the symbol of choice

Why did God give man and woman a choice? Because God did not want robots, even in the garden. He created man and woman with the ability to choose.

Now, in His sovereignty, God knew what the man and woman's choice would be. Yet, in His wisdom, He gave the ability to choose whether to obey Him or to disobey Him.

God wanted a relationship, even back in the garden with Adam and Eve. A relationship is a two-way street – they would love Him and He would love them.

This tree, of course, was the test and, as you know, after man ate, he was kept from the tree of life. I always wondered why. I think perhaps I have discovered the answer – because of what it represented. Adam and Eve had eaten of this tree, therefore becoming sinners. If they had then eaten the tree of life, they would have lived forever confined in their wicked state.

One of the blessings that God has given us is death. We will not live forever as sinners. Forgiven as we are, it would be a tragic thing to live forever like we live today. Death will open the gate to heaven where we will be given glorified, perfect bodies and our souls will match the Savior's in its perfection.

So God kept them from that and then, gave them another symbol – the symbol of forgiveness. In the coats that He gave them to wear, the animals died evidently in atonement for their sin; the blood of the animals was shed.

The Sculpturing of Eve (Genesis 2:18-23)

Go on to Genesis 2:18a, God's first statement of displeasure.

Then the Lord God said, . . .

(note God's displeasure for the first time),

. . . "It is not good for man to be alone; . . ."

What struck me about this verse was the fact that man was living in a perfect environment. He has a perfect occupation – one that he loves. He gets up in the morning ready to go; ready to take care of the garden. He has a perfect relationship, as perfect as it can be with God. He communes with God and God sums all of this up and says, "It is not good . . .".

So God, in His perfect timing, plans to create a woman. What I like about God is His timing. He did not rush up to Adam, and say, "Adam, you need a wife. I'm going to create one for you."

Adam would have said, "I need a what? I need a wife? I'm not so sure I do."

Then God, as a perfect matchmaker, sets him up.

Will you notice what God does in the next few verses. Look at verse 19a,

Out of the ground the Lord God formed every beast . . .

Now see that God, in verse 18b, has already decided to make him a mate.

. . . I will make him a helper suitable for him.

He has not told Adam yet. But first, in Genesis 2:19b-20a, He,

. . . formed every beast of the field and every bird of the sky, and brought them to the man, . . .

(obviously in pairs),

. . . to see what he would call them; and whatever the man called a living creature, that was its name. The man gave the names to all the cattle, and to the birds of the sky, and to every beast of the field, . . .

Here is Adam, just naming them off. Here comes two more and he, in his brilliance, notes the characteristics. In fact, the original text gives the implication that he gave them names matching their characteristics. He was brilliant and he is naming all of them. Then, Adam comes to the very end, and almost as if it were his thought, in verse 20b,

. . . but for Adam there was not found a helper suitable for him.

In other words, Adam is starting to look now. He has named a few hundred animals and is now on the lookout, "Let's see. There is only one of me and there are two of them."

What is God doing? He is setting him up! He is making Adam come to the point where he realizes he is alone; he does not have the other half. Then, in verses 21 and 22a,

So the Lord God caused a deep sleep to fall upon the man, and he slept; then He took one of his ribs and closed up the flesh at that place. The Lord God fashioned into a woman the rib which He had taken from the man, . . .

Now, the word translated "fashioned," in verse 22, "The Lord God fashioned" or "formed," is different than that used when God formed man. This word is a beautiful word that could be translated "sculptured". It is as if God, as any master who would paint a beautiful portrait, knelt over that rib, that flesh, and sculpted a beautiful woman – one who would become the counterpart of Adam.

The importance of the rib

We need to answer the question, "Why the rib? Why was it the rib that God took to fashion or sculpt a woman?" Let me give three reasons.

1. To show the unity of the human race

We all come from Adam. This is a tremendous theological truth that will come out in our study of the book of Romans. Because we are all in and out of and from Adam, we are all sinners; we all have Adam's nature. But the second Adam will come, who is Jesus Christ. And we who are in Him, the second Adam, will be forgiven. So this truth will be revealed later in the New Testament and is a beautiful theological truth.

2. To guarantee the dignity of woman kind

Woman is not made from an inferior substance. She is made from the same thing that man is made from. Do not picture in your mind that God just took a bone, a rib? He actually took flesh and blood around that rib. He took a chunk, as it were, and fashioned her in the same substance He had used to create the man.

3. To illustrate the closest of kinship

God did not take a bone from the foot, as you may have read or heard, as if man would tread upon her; as if man were above her. God did not take something from his head, as if she was to be superior or above him. God did not take a bone from Adams's hand, as if she was to be a servant of man and do his work. God took a bone from his side, to illustrate the closest of companionship. She would be by his side. She would serve as queen of the garden, of paradise, and Adam would serve as king. We will develop this further in our next discussion.

I love the next part, in verses 22 through 23a,

The Lord God fashioned into a woman the rib which He had taken from the man, and brought her to the man. The man said, This is now bone of my bones, and flesh of my flesh; . . .

Now just use your imagination in this. I really do not think this was the first thing Adam said. The text does not say this is the first thing Adam said. I think the first thing that happened was man probably looked at his counterpart and said, "Wow!"

This is the first time man whistled in the history of mankind! What a beautiful lady. And then, I think they probably talked for hours, as if they were long lost best friends. I think what is happening in verse 23 is that the man is introducing her to all of the other creatures. It is as if he says, "Now listen up. "This is now . . .

(in fact, the literal Hebrew can be translated, "This is now *at last*...*),

"...bone of my bone, flesh of my flesh; . . .". Continue to verse 23b,

. . . she shall be called Woman, because she was taken out of Man.

I believe that this was the introduction of woman to everything that God had created.

Application

This is as far as we are going to go in the text today. Let me apply a couple of things that strike me from this chapter.

Genesis 2:1-23

1. The garden of Eden – a place where mankind would choose who he would obey

The first application is found in the garden of Eden itself. The garden of Eden, men and women, would represent a place where mankind would choose who he would obey – the tempter or the creator.

It reminds me of another garden where Jesus Christ struggled with the will of His Father. We are told in Luke 22, that He sweat drops as if they were blood. And finally, in verse 42b, He said, in the agony of His soul,

. . . not My will, but Yours be done.

No, we are not in the garden of Eden and we are not in Gethsemane, but ladies and gentlemen, I believe you and I are in a garden, as it were. We are in a place of choosing who we will follow, who we will obey – the tempter or the creator.

2. The tree – symbol of the choice of eternal healing through Christ or eternal death

The garden is not the only thing in this chapter that points to Jesus Christ – a tree does also. A tree has been used throughout scripture to symbolize some powerful truths. The tree in the garden represented choice.

Another time, when Moses was in the wilderness, the children of Israel were being very rebellious. We are told in Numbers 21, that God sent poisonous vipers to bite them. He then told Moses to make a serpent and lift it up on a tree, and whoever would look at the tree would be healed. That represented healing, and those who looked were healed.

Of course I also think of Calvary. I Peter 2:24, records,

and He Himself bore our sins in His body on the cross [tree], so that we might die to sin and live to righteousness; for by His wounds you were healed.

My friend there is a tree in your life as well. You either stand before the tree called Calvary as a forgiven individual or you stand before it as an unrepentant unbeliever. The tree is lifted up today bearing Christ, and it is ours to choose. We may choose to accept Him; to accept that atonement as our own; to take Him as our personal savior.

54

The Climax of Creation

The Climax of Creation

Genesis 2:1-23

Digging Deeper :

God had created the earth, the sun, the trees and the animals. He spoke and these things came into being. But, now, God creates man. Instead of speaking man into existence, God **makes** man. This change must mean that man is different than the animals and the trees. Man is something special to God.

> Genesis 1:27 *God created man in His own image, in the image of God He created him; male and female He created them.*

1) What does it mean to be created "in the image of God"?

_____

_____

_____

_____

God took great care in making man. He took a lump of ground and formed a **perfect** man. Man had no imperfections before the "fall." Then this man was brought to life by God's own breath.

> Genesis 2:7 *Then the Lord God formed man of dust from the ground, and breathed into his nostrils the breath of life; and man became a living being.*

2) What is the breath of life?

_____

Yes, God breathed an immortal soul into man. The soul will live forever – whether in heaven or in hell.

> Genesis 2:8-9 *The Lord God planted a garden toward the east, in Eden, and there He placed the man whom He had formed. Out of the ground the Lord caused to grow every tree that is pleasing to the sight and good for food; the tree of life also in the midst of the garden, and the tree of the knowledge of good and evil.*

God placed two trees in the garden. One represents **immortality** and the other represents **choice.** The tree of life would give man immortality. We would live forever. But man chose to sin. So, with immortality, man would be an immortal, sinful being. We would live forever in our sinful, wicked state. But, God gave the gift of forgiveness. The animal skins that He gave to Adam and Eve represented the shedding of blood for their forgiveness. Thus, one day we all would be able to enter into God's presence by the shedding of the blood of His Son.

3) The tree of knowledge represents man's ability to choose between good and evil. Discuss why an all powerful God would give man the ability to choose.

_____

_____

_____

_____

_____

Adam and Eve chose to eat from the forbidden tree and thus brought sin into the perfect world that God had created. God has given us a choice – repent of our sins, trust in Jesus and give our whole self to Him. This is the only way that we can one day return to the perfect place that is in God's presence.

Genesis 2:22a *The Lord God fashioned into a woman the rib which He had taken from the man, . . .*

4) Explain 3 reasons that it is important that Eve be made from Adam's rib.

_____

_____

_____

_____

_____

_____

5) How does Eve being created from the same substance as Adam illustrate the equality of man and woman in God's eyes?

_____

_____

_____

_____

Romans 5:12 *Therefore, just as through one man sin entered into the world, and death through sin, and so death spread to all men, because all sinned--*

Romans 5:17 *For if by the transgression of the one, death reigned through the one, much more those who receive the abundance of grace and of the gift of righteousness will reign in life through the One, Jesus Christ.*

Romans 5:19 *For as through the one man's disobedience the many were made sinners, even so through the obedience of the One the many will be made righteous.*

Take It To Heart :

God allowed Adam to be tempted in the garden of Eden

Through one man's disobedience the many were made sinners

God allowed Jesus to be tempted in Gethsemane.

Through the obedience of the One the many will be made righteous

You are in that garden of choice. Who will you follow, the tempter or the creator?

Luke 22:42b *... not My will, but Yours be done.*

59

God's Design for Marriage

Genesis 2:23-25

Introduction

Turn in your Bible to Genesis, chapters 1 and 2, as we continue our study of this book. In Genesis, chapter 1, we have discovered the amazing truths of the perfectly designed creation of God – especially in our last discussion, while looking at the human body. We learned that over and over and over again, as God saw what He had made,

. . . God saw that it was good . . .

God saw and, "It was good! It was good! It was good! It was very good!" – as He summarized the six days of creation. However, in chapter 2, verse 18a,

Then the Lord God said, "It is not good for the man to be alone . . ."

Then God says, "But something is not good –and that is that man is alone." And He says, in verse 18b,

. . . I will make a helper suitable for him.

The name Adam comes from the Hebrew word that means "earth". God created man out of earth. The same chemical elements that make up mankind are in the ground. He then takes a portion of Adam's side and creates, or literally sculpts, a woman. "He will build her" is the literal translation of the Hebrew words.

If your translation reads "a helpmeet," then draw a line between the words "help" and "meet". These are two Hebrew words that could be translated literally, "a helper suitable". They mean, "one who complements; one who fills up the empty spaces of man; one who fits". Note, it is not "one who gives fits," it is "one who is fit to". In fact, the Hebrew, I recently discovered, could literally be translated in this fashion, "one answering back to". But do not take that too literally!God knew exactly what He was doing when He sculpted into existence the first woman, Eve. He introduces her to man in verse 22 of chapter 2.

The Lord God fashioned into a woman the rib which He had taken from the man, and brought her to the man.

And the man caught his breath – that is in between the lines! I think it took him a while before he could speak. In fact, I think perhaps they talked for hours, until finally, as we previously discussed, Adam makes an introduction of this woman to the rest of creation. In verse 23a, He perhaps stands up, quiets the animals, and says, "Look,"

. . . This is now bone of my bones, and flesh of my flesh . . .

After the word "now," the words "at last!" could be inserted. Adam is literally saying, "This is now, at last, finally, bone of my bone, and flesh of my flesh. I now have, at last, a counterpart, one answering to, one who will fill up the void. Flesh of my flesh!"

Adam continues in verse 23b,

. . . she shall be called Woman, because she was taken out of Man.

Principles of the Marriage Relationship

Now, in our discussion today, I want to give some principles relating to the marriage relationship. These are taken from the text and will make the marital relationship firm and enduring. They still apply today and are as powerful and as timely as they were centuries ago. It is interesting that God will move directly into this after introducing Eve to Adam.

1. The Principle of Consideration

Look at Genesis 2:24a,

For this reason a man shall leave his father and his mother, ...

Now understand that God, in this verse, is not speaking in reference to the relationship with the mother and father. In fact, wise is the individual who recognizes when he or she gets married that it is really two worlds merging into one larger one. The relationships of your wife or husband are brought into that marriage and become your relationships. So, at that point, you are involved with uncles and aunts, nieces and nephews, mothers and dads-in-law, brothers and sisters-in-law, perhaps sons and daughters, and all of these are involved in this larger world.

God is not saying to abandon your mother and father, which is a literal translation of the word leave. He is not saying to abandon them in terms of your relationship with them – that is going to continue. In fact, you are creating relationships with another family; another entire world.

God is also not referring, ladies and gentlemen, to the sense of responsibility. We do not abandon our sense of responsibility toward our father and mother. In fact, Jesus' harshest words were toward the Pharisees who were abandoning their parents in taking care of them in their aged state (Mark 7). They were hoarding their finances so that moms and dads who were unable to take care of themselves were left alone and were in poverty. The Pharisees were saying, "Well, we've dedicated this money to God, so we can't give it away."

Jesus Christ pointed a finger through their façade and said, "If you cannot take care of them, you are not religious. In fact, you don't even know God."

God, in this passage, is not referring to abandoning a relationship or the responsibility. So, what does He mean when He talks of leaving? Let me give what I think He is saying.

God is referring to priority; to the sense of direction. So, a man and a woman leave the nest and create for themselves their own purpose; their own direction. Their marital relationship takes priority over any other relationship. The responsibility to the wife or husband now has priority over every other relationship in existence. No human relationship then, ladies and gentlemen, should have priority over your marital relationship.

This means that you may strike out on a different course than Mom and Dad would want. You may try some things that they may never try. You may go places that they might never go.

I think this verse also involves the parents of those who marry. This is the painful part because this means that fathers will have to suffer the pain of knowing their little daughters are now looking to another man. I get choked up thinking about it. Can you imagine what it will be like? When my little girls marry – forty years from now? They are going to look toward another man for strength and guidance. It is great being first place in their little lives. I love it! But there is going to come a day when they are going to say, "Dad, I want to introduce you to this guy. He now is my life; my world."

He will be unworthy, of course! And, there will come a day when I may hear that they have purchased an automobile that I do not think is a good deal. The temptation for all dads is to just march over there and give them that lecture. You know, the one on Fiscal Responsibility 332. But you have to bite your tongue, because they have to learn.

One difficulty, I have been told, is that many couples live with their parents' values in mind, rather than formulating their own. You may be married and afraid to develop your own direction; your own values, because more than anything in the world, you want to hear Dad say, "You're doing a great job!" and you want to hear Mom say, "I'm pleased with your direction."

Do you know what God says? God says that what your parents say is now secondary. You, as husband and wife, together are to strive to hear *Him* say, "I'm pleased!"

It means, moms, that your son is now going to be cared for by a woman of different tastes. You know he does not like to eat that food, but you had better not tell her – let her find out. You know how he likes to have his shirts washed and pressed, do not dare advise – let that girl find out for herself.

What I am suggesting is that this message of abandonment is not just for the husband and wife – it is also for the parents. And the message is, "Let them go!!" In fact, you will be doing a great service to your young people, if you will allow them to develop their own values, priorities, and direction.

There are several periods in a marriage, I have read and have experienced a few of them, of course, that create a tremendous amount of stress on a marriage - the first few years and the birth of a child, to name a couple. It is in those situations that moms and dads who watch their married kids can really help their direction. When that daughter comes to you and says, "Dad, I don't know what to do."

You could ask her, "Did you ask your husband? What does he think?"

When your son says, "Mom, I'm not sure what I should do in this situation."

Your response could be, "Did you ask your wife?"

It is in times such as these that parents can have a tremendous impact in developing the direction of their young people. I know it is hard to let go. I will discover that one day. Some of you could tell me by experience.

I cannot believe this is true and you probably will not believe it either, but I read recently of a situation where a mother did not want to let go of her newlywed son. This mother called her son three times on his wedding night! Now that is kind of funny, but I thought about it and wondered, what kind of mother would call her son on his wedding night? Then, I thought about it a little longer and wondered what kind of dummy would leave his phone on the hook?

God is saying, in the first manual on marriage, that your marital relationship takes priority. It may mean disagreeing with mom and dad at times. It may mean taking a different direction and establishing different values. But the marital relationship takes priority. That is the principle of considering that wife above all other women; that husband above all other men; above all other relationships. That is the principle of consideration.

2. The Principle of Commitment

Let me give the second key principle that I see in this text. It is found in the word "cleave," and is the principle of commitment. Look again at chapter 2, verse 24, at the second part of the verse.

For this reason a man shall leave his father and mother, and be joined [cleave] to his wife; . . .

The word "cleave" could be literally translated, "weld or grip".

The marital scene in America today would change drastically if couples would come into marriage with one basic proposition – that there is absolutely no way out! As one man wrote, "Commitment is taking your hand off the doorknob to the back door of your marriage."

There is no way out, but there is a way through. If you have in your marriage a fire escape, there will come a time when you are going to run for it. So, you had better seal it up.

Fulfilling marriage involves three commitments

One man wrote that there are three very important commitments in marriage. In fact, these are right out of Scripture. Let me give these three commitments that are important in a marriage and are included in this principle of commitment. They involve three relationships.

A. The commitment between you and the Lord

If you are going to have the principle of commitment in your marriage, it means you are committed to the Lord. This is crucial. Before you ever talk about a relationship with another human being, talk about your relationship with God. The reason for this, husbands, is that there is no way in the world that you could ever love your wife without first understanding and experiencing the love of Jesus Christ. How else are you to love your wife like Christ loved the church (Ephesians 5:25)?

B. The commitment between your spouse and the Lord

You had better encourage it. Bless your heart if you get in the way of your spouse's relationship with the Lord. God help you if your spouse has to wake you up and get you out of the bed in the morning to go to church. You are hindering the potential relationship. If your breakfast is late because she or he is reading God's word, *fantastic*! Encourage that relationship that they have with the Lord.

A young man walked into my office recently, and asked if I would perform his wedding. He had never attended this church. In fact, I had never seen him before. So, I just asked him a few questions about his relationship with the Lord. It was nonexistent.

I explained to him the truth. I said, "Look, how can the Lord not be involved in your marriage? He is the One who designed your marriage. He is the One who has the manual for it. In fact, if you build it without the Lord, according to David, in Psalm 127:1, you are going to labor in vain."

He was not very interested. I shocked the daylights out of him by looking him in the eye and saying, "Look, man, why don't you just skip the marriage and live with your girlfriend?"

"What? What are you suggesting that for?"

I simply told him, "Since God's idea is marriage, and since God is not a part of your marriage, He's not going to be involved. Why worry with appearances? Having a ceremony in a church is absolutely meaningless. You want it your way, do it your way. But if you want to do it God's way, then God has to be involved. You need a right relationship with Jesus Christ if you're ever going to pull it off. Your spouse needs to have a right relationship with the Lord if you are to ever experience the kind of commitment He wants."

C. The commitment between you and your spouse

Notice that I placed this relationship last. That is because it hangs upon the balance of the other two. Show me a woman who is out of fellowship with Jesus Christ, and I will show you a woman who is out of fellowship with her husband. Show me a man who is in rebellion to the word of God, and I will show you a man who is impossible to live with. Marriage hangs upon the first two commitments being in proper perspective.

A respected professor of mine said that eighty-five percent of his marital counseling, as a man who has been teaching God's word for nearly forty years, involves a man or woman who walks into his office and says these words, "I'm not getting out of my marriage what I deserve."

He knows that they are already in phase three in the deterioration of the marriage. That is when spouses begin to concentrate on "I, me, my," and never say the words "we, us".

How could we ever circumvent the selfish nature of our own being? By having a relationship with Jesus Christ and learning to die to self and to live to Him. Then we can live in the proper perspective of our horizontal relationship.

3. The Principle of Companionship

Look at verses 24 and 25.

For this reason a man shall leave his father and mother, and be joined to his wife; and they shall become one flesh. And the man and his wife were both naked and were not ashamed.

Now this union obviously involved physical intimacy, but it involves much more. That is why I call this the principle of companionship. It also involves spiritual, emotional, and mental unity. It involves two people going in the same direction. That is the principle of companionship.

One man writes that this involves the complete identification of one personality with the other in a community of interests and pursuits.

Genesis 2:23-25

Do you know what is happening today? People get married and the husband goes this way and the wife goes that way. They go in separate directions after separate pursuits. Days off are spent alone. There is no pursuit of developing this companionship. At night, when they are together, the television is on and very little conversation takes place. Then, they separate to go to work, come home tired, and the day off is for themselves.

I want to say something that may shock you, but I believe it is true. I believe many husbands and wives today are lonely. I believe an evaluation of most marriages in America would find the missing ingredient of companionship; would find husbands and wives who are lonely. It is possible to live under the same roof with someone and still not have a companion; still not have that close friend that God designed.

One clinic took a survey and found that nearly ninety-five percent of those interviewed expressed that they did not feel close to their mate. That is sad. Do you know why that is so sad? Because the basis, the first thing that God said He would do for man was alleviate loneliness. Man is lonely and that is not good. And on the basis of that, He built someone, He formulated, created, sculpted someone who would fill in the void, fill the need, answer back to, complement.

Isn't it interesting, my friends, that when God sought to alleviate the loneliness of man, He did not create ten good friends? He created a woman; a wife.

Now that implies something, men and women. Let me speak to just the men for a moment. If you are bored and lonely today, the solution is not a hobby – the solution is not a bag of golf clubs; the solution is not another friend. The solution is developing a companionship, a warm and vital friendship with your wife.

Ladies, if you are lonely today, do you know what the solution is that is implied in this text? You are to develop a companionship with your husband; a warm and vital friendship with the man that God intended to fill in your void and lonely places.

Three ways to develop marital companionship

Let me give three ways to develop companionship in your marriage; three words that will develop companionship with your spouse.

1. Confidence

Confidence is a key ingredient to developing companionship with your spouse. Turn to Proverbs 17:9, which says,

He who conceals a transgression seeks love, but he who repeats a matter separates intimate friends.

Who is separated? "Intimate friends" or companions.

The longer you live with your spouse, the more you will understand and know their weaknesses, faults, and shortcomings. That is information that God intended for you to know. So many times, however, when couples argue, the first thing that comes out is something that is used as a weapon directed at one of the weaknesses.

For instance, a man may open up to his wife and admit to her that he is incapable of or finding it difficult to handle finances. The next time they have an argument, guess what comes out? "You never have a penny in your pocket."

What do you think happens after that? He is going to clam up.

A wife may admit to her husband that she really feels intimidated about being compared to her mother. Oh boy! We have got a weapon now. When the next argument erupts and reaches a peak, out comes, "You're just like your mother!"

Guess what – you have just broken confidence.

Wives, sometimes you know things about your husbands that you share with other ladies at work. And men, you share things about your wives with other men at work. My friends, you are destroying the potential for companionship – because there is no confidence; because you cannot trust each other.

Solomon says, in this Proverbs verse, that in order to have companionship or confidence, you must cover transgressions and not repeat them.

2. Communication

Let me give you two thoughts concerning communication. All of these begin with "C's," so hopefully, we will be able to remember them a little more easily.

A. Communication through confrontation

You might say, "Wait a second, I thought I wasn't supposed to criticize my spouse."

I am not suggesting that you be critical, but let me turn your attention to Proverbs, chapter 27, to look at what Solomon says. Now, you might say that the reason you never say anything to your mate is because you love them; the reason that you never confront them about something is because you love them. And aren't you just supposed to accept everything?

Well, what does Proverbs 27:5-6, say?

Better is open rebuke than love that is concealed. Faithful are the wounds of a friend, but deceitful are the kisses of an enemy.

In other words, the wounds of rebuke are more productive in developing character than the kisses of an enemy, which are deceitful.

I have seen couples where the wife does not say a word; where she is the model of passivity. Some husbands might say, "Well, I'd like to learn the secret of that one."

No, you would not. The reason you would not is because of what happened behind closed doors, behind the scenes. It may have even happened out in the open. The wife suggested something to the husband, and *bang*, "Don't you give me advice. I'm the commander of this ship."

The husband has squelched the potential confrontation that would ultimately sharpen him. The same is true of the husband advising the wife, but I have seen it more with wives advising husbands. The husbands do not want to hear it and would rather their wives remain silent. And yet, they have been robbed of one of the best things a marriage provides. That is a sharpening impact of that mate toward you in confronting you with things that you cannot see; that you are blind to.

I read a story that is kind of humorous and yet, it is not. A husband and wife were celebrating their fiftieth wedding anniversary. Everyone always admired their relationship because she was just the kindest thing and he could do just about anything he wanted to do and she would never say a word. They asked her one day, "How did this happen? What's your secret?"

She replied, "Well, it happened on our honeymoon. We went to the Grand Canyon and were taking two mules down the side of the Grand Canyon. My husband's mule stumbled, and he grabbed him by the ears and shook him and said, 'That's once.' A few yards further, the mule stumbled again and my husband took him by the ears and said, 'That's twice.' Finally, the third time the mule stumbled, my husband got off the mule, got out a pistol, and shot the mule. I started to protest, but he ran over to me, grabbed me by the ears and said, 'That's once.'"

Would you look at Proverbs 27:17? If this isn't talking about the marital relationship, I don't know what is.

Iron sharpens iron, so one man sharpens another.

The spouse, the mate that God has given you is iron. Someone said that a good marriage creates enough friction that it is like sandpaper in rounding off the rough edges. That is what this verse is talking about when it says, "Iron sharpens iron".

Husbands, when you cause your wives to clam up, and wives, when you are advised by your husbands on something you cannot see and you respond, "I don't want to hear that," you have drawn lines around your marriages. You have seen it, perhaps you have been involved in it – there is a line and, buddy, don't step across that line. If you do, you're on my turf. That's mine and don't say anything about that. As a result, you have a blind spot in your life that your mate cannot help you with because you refuse to hear. Confrontation is crucial and sharpening.

B. Communication through counsel

Look at Proverbs 27:9. I like this verse.

Oil and perfume make the heart glad, so a man's counsel is sweet to his friend.

God has given the husband and wife an excellent source of objective wisdom. In fact, I think a marriage is strong when the couple is literally counseling one another.

Now, when you, as a husband, want advice and ask your wife and she responds, do not say, "Well, that's kind of dumb. I'll do it my way after all."

No, accept the counsel. Solomon says the counsel is sweet. I think he implies, of course, in this verse, that the attitude in which we counsel our mate and as well, the attitude in which we confront our mate, is sweet. Confronting is never intended to tear down. It is always intended to build up.

Now, you may think, "Well, my wife never listens to my counsel," or, "My husband never listens to my advice." Perhaps you should look at the way you give it. Is it sweet like perfume? Is it laced with love?

So, in order to develop companionship, we need confidence and communication.

C. Caring

The word "care" comes from the Gothic root that means, "to lament, to grieve". Isn't it interesting that we get our word "care" from that? Why? Because to lament, or to grieve is to be emotionally involved with the effects, the situation, and the life of another human being. So, if I am to care for my spouse, that means I am emotionally involved in that which hurts, that which helps, that which brings joy into his or her life.

Caring is the tangible expression of love. Love in intangible. You can say, "I love my mate," until you are blue in the face, but until you make tangible expressions by caring – which might include taking the garbage out, washing the dishes, sending a card or writing a note, calling on the phone unexpectedly – it has no meaning. Caring is the tangible expression of love such as these, and that develops companionship.

Conclusion

I think we could best illustrate marriage by watching a child learn to walk. It has been a joyful thing to see my children learn to walk. Many of you have seen it happen.

First, they sit on the ground and all of a sudden, they get the bright idea to start crawling. After a while, they get down on their hands and knees, but they do not have the motor running yet. They just kind of sit there and rock back and forth. Finally, the motor starts and they start crawling all over the house.

Then, they get the idea that, "Hey, there's a couch over there. If I crawl over to the couch, maybe I can pull myself up and stand up like my dad or mom or brother or sister."

And would you believe it, they finally pull themselves up and they are standing. Boy, the celebration begins. You break out the camera. You take thirty-five shots. Ten years later, you wonder, "What are all those shots of this little kid standing at the couch?" But that was when it happened.

Finally, the child sees dad or mom sitting across the living room floor and they think, "It'd be great if I could walk across to them."

And do you know what happens? They take their first step. Bang! And they sit there awhile, and they think, "Well, let's back up and try that again."

So, they take a couple of steps. Over a process of days and weeks, although after they start walking, you wish it had taken years, but they finally take two or three steps into your open arms. You rejoice and have another celebration. They have learned to walk!

No matter how long you have been walking though, you always have the capacity to stumble and fall. No matter how long you have been married, you pull yourself up, you take a step, and bang, you fall. Then, you pull yourself up again and walk a couple of steps, and you fall again, you blow it. Now, wouldn't it be foolish for that child to sit on the floor, after trying about five hundred times, and say, "Well, Dad, I guess I'm not called to walk."

So many couples fall and stumble and get up and fall again, and then, some may come to the conclusion, "Well, I guess God doesn't want us to walk together."

My friend, when you fall and stumble, and you will, because you will always have the capacity, the difference will be that you are developing a relationship. Build into it the principles of consideration, commitment, companionship.

Where do we start? First of all, we start with our relationship to the Lord. Then we stop with our relationship with our spouse. We leave it up to the Lord how they will respond, but we do what is right.

May our marriages be characterized with the ingredients: consideration, commitment, companionship, confidence, counsel, and caring.

God's Design for Marriage

Genesis 2:23-25

Digging Deeper :

Marriage should be the merging of two worlds together. Two worlds will come together that can make the total union stronger. Each family will have new aunts and uncles, cousins and nephews. This new, bigger family must come together. Genesis 2:24 tells that a man will leave his father and mother. This does not instruct newly weds to abandon their parents. A married couple should not ignore their parents. They should support their parents, just as each member of a family should support the others. God designed marriage to give the new husband and wife a new priority and a new commitment in their lives. This new priority is the new commitment to their marriage and to each other. The priority to the husband or to the wife has to be first over any other human relationship.

Genesis 2: 24a *For this reason a man shall leave his father and his mother ...*

---

1) What is the responsibility of the parents when their children get married?

_____

_____

_____

_____

If the parents cling to their children, once they are married, the children will not be allowed to set their own direction. The direction of their marriage will be that of their parents. This can cause problems in the marriage.

74

Genesis 2:24b *and be joined [cleave] to his wife . . .*

Ephesians 5:25   *Husbands, love your wives, just as Christ also loved the church and gave Himself up for her.*

2) Compare the two verses above.

_____

_____

_____

_____

The word "join" or "cleave" in Genesis 2:24 means to **cling to, join with, and stay with**. All these are good meanings at many times during the course of a marriage. When a husband and a wife are joined together, it is God's intent for them to stay together. This can only be done through love for God and each other.

How did Christ "love" the church? – The answer to that question can be found in the Greek words used for "love." In his book, The Four Loves, C.S. Lewis discusses four Greek words for love. The first Greek word is "storge". This is the affection that we have for near relatives. The second word for love is "philia". This describes friendship. Thirdly, there is "eros", which is the love between a man and a woman. The greatest love of all is "Agape". Agape is the word used in Ephesians 5:25. It is a Christian love. God loves – "Agape" – the church with the greatest love possible. Christ was willing to give His life for the church. With the imperative form of the word in Ephesians 5:25, God commands husbands to have this "Agape" love for their wives. Husband must love their wives with the greatest love possible. Husbands must love their wives with a love greater than they love themselves, just as Christ loved the church. Husbands must love their wives with a Christian love. Not only did Christ love the church, He was "head" of the church. Husbands are commanded to be the head of the family, just as Christ is head of the church. Husbands, do not take this headship lightly.

Psalms 127:1a *Unless the Lord builds the house, They labor in vain who build it...*

3) How are a "solid marriage" and a "commitment to the Lord" complimentary?

_____

_____

_____

_____

Proverbs 27:5-6a *Better is open rebuke than love that is concealed. Faithful are the wounds of a friend, but deceitful are the kisses of an enemy.*

4) How does confrontation between husband and wife strengthen a marriage?

_____

_____

_____

5) Love is intangible. Caring is a tangible expression of love. Name several ways that a person can care for their spouse.

_____

_____

_____

_____

_____

Take It To Heart :

Why is confidence between spouses important? Your spouse will know things about you that nobody else knows or that anybody else should know. Your spouse will know the deep secret things that trouble you, or that are your greatest fears. What each spouse does with this knowledge yields a level of confidence.

Does your spouse have confidence in you?

Does the confidence your spouse have in you need to be improved?

Name three ways that you can improve the confidence between you and your spouse.

How does confidence and companionship compliment each other?

Goodbye to Paradise

Genesis 3

Introduction

We discovered in our last discussion of Genesis, chapter 2, that God created a beautiful relationship between husband and wife. No sooner had God created that relationship than Satan set the wheels in motion to destroy it. And, we will find in Genesis 3, the tragic fall of man.

I think Genesis 3, is the saddest, most tragic chapter in all of the Bible. Yet, as we study this chapter today, we will find interwoven into its tragic tapestry, the threads of hope and salvation.

In Genesis 3:1a, we are told,

Now the serpent was more crafty than any beast of the field which the Lord God had made. . . .

Oh, Satan is indeed crafty. In fact, two times we are warned of Satan in scriptures by the apostles.

In II Corinthians 2:11, Paul exhorts the church in Corinth,

so that no advantage would be taken of us by Satan, for we are not ignorant of his schemes.

In other words, we are not to be ignorant of Satan's schemes. The word "scheme" is the original word "agnumen," which means, "mindset or mentality". Satan has a mentality, a mindset, a way of thinking, and I think he would discover that type of thinking in the humanistic philosophy of today's society.

Paul will also warn the church in Ephesians 6:11, to,

Put on the full armor of God, so that you will be able to stand firm against the schemes of the devil.

The word "schemes," or it may be "wiles" in your translation, comes from a different original word. It is the word "methodios," from which we get our word "method".

So, we discover from the writings of scripture that Satan has a mindset, a mentality, and he also has a method. We will discover in Genesis 3, the methodology of Satan and its five-faceted deception.

Satan's Five-fold Deceit in Tempting Eve

1. Satan appeared in a form to deceive

Look again at verse 1a.

Now the serpent was more crafty than any beast of the field which the Lord God had made. . . .

Evidently, Satan took the form of the serpent. This was one of the creations of God and it was beautiful.

Now understand that this was before the fall. The serpent, like any being or beast, had a wonderful relationship with mankind. It was a beautiful thing and its skin gave off beautiful colors. So, there was no need to fear. Perhaps the beautiful colors were attractive to the woman, so Satan chose to inhabit the serpent.

Satan inhabited a serpent because he wanted to take a form that would deceive. You need to understand that he is not running around town wearing a bright, red suit with a long tail, carrying a pitchfork, showing fangs, and shoveling coal. He is an angel of light. He will take whatever appearance necessary in order to deceive. With Eve, it was the form of a serpent.

Satan displayed cunning in two ways

I want to point out Satan's cunning ways. I asked myself the question, when I looked at verse 1, "Why did Satan come to Eve alone? Why did he pick on her?" I think his cunning is revealed in two ways.

A. Satan understood the pattern of God's creation

Satan was there and knew that woman was created the weaker vessel. He understood that she was the one easily led, the one prone to follow. So he was cunning in coming to her.

B. Satan understood the principle of divide and conquer

He came to Eve when she was all alone. Ecclesiastes 4:9-12a.

Two are better than one because they have a good return for their labor. For if either of them falls, the one will lift up his companion. But woe to the one who falls when there is not another to lift him up. Furthermore, if two lie down together they keep warm, but how can one be warm alone?

(notice this phrase in verse 12a),

And if one can overpower him who is alone, two can resist him. . . .

Satan understood the principle of dividing and conquering.

I believe we find in this, an emphasis on the necessity of mutual accountability in marriage. The importance for mutual accountability and unity in marriage is discovered in this temptation of Eve. I think you will find that a person, who is unwilling to live in unity with their spouse, is unwilling to follow the guidelines of the word of God in relation to her or him.

The individual who is in rebellion to the institution of the local New Testament church; who is ostracizing himself from the fellowship, from institutions that God has ordained; who is living apart from unity in that relationship, is a person who is a susceptible person. I think that person is a "sitting duck".

There is an interesting verse that the apostle Peter gives us when he talks about husbands and wives living in unity together. I Peter 3:7b.

. . . so that your prayers will not be hindered.

That has a fascinating implication. He is implying that, if you as a husband and wife, are not in a harmonious relationship, your prayers are being hindered.

Let me suggest something startling. If you are at odds with your husband or wife, you might as well not pray. It does not matter if you get up at four o'clock in the morning. If you are at odds with your husband or wife, God is interested in the prayer of confession. He is interested in the harmonious relationship between husband and wife. So, forget the religious façade. Get it right with your spouse, and then pray. Then your prayers will not be hindered – God can answer.

2. Satan cast doubt on the word of God

Look at the last part of Genesis 3:1.

And he said to the woman, "Indeed, has God said, 'You shall not eat from any tree of the garden?'"

He casually suggests, "Eve, has God said this?" And, if a serpent can smile, he smiled. He says, "Do you really think God meant you couldn't eat from every tree?"

Understand that Satan is not coming across as some brash, rude character. Shakespeare said it well when he wrote, "The prince of darkness is a gentleman."

The serpent came in to beguile her and asked a simple polite question, "Did God say that?"

However, he was sowing in her mind, a seed of doubt.

Notice the response of woman in Genesis 3:2, 3.

The woman said to the serpent, "From the fruit of the trees of the garden we may eat; but from the fruit of the tree which is in the middle of the garden, God has said, 'You shall not eat from it or touch it, . . .

(God did not say that – He only said they could not eat it),

"'. . . or you will die.'"

3. Satan denied the truth of God's word

Look at verse 4, and notice that now he is a little brash.

The serpent said to the woman, "You surely shall not die!"

Ladies and gentlemen, every temptation is an opportunity to either believe the words of Satan or the words of God. God said, in Genesis 2: 17b,

. . . eat from it you will surely die.

Satan said,

. . . You surely shall not die.

Understand, men and women, that when you sin, you are either believing the words of God or the lies of Satan. God always tells the truth. In John 8:44b, Jesus declares,

. . . [Satan is] the father of lies.

One of the things Satan will do, as he did with Eve, is pull you from the words of God, sow seeds of doubt in your mind about the words of God, so that you will one day, deny the words of God and follow the words of Satan.

4. Satan attributed evil motives to God

Look at the first part of Genesis 3:5. This is the amazing thing about the entire temptation to me. Satan suggests; he dares to imply,

For God knows that in the day you eat from it, your eyes will be opened, . . .

Now, it is God who is jealous. It is God who is the one who in a cowardly manner, protects His throne. Satan would suggest to the woman, "Look, if you eat, God is afraid. He knows that you will be like Him and He trembles at that thought. He is an envious God. He is jealous of His character."

Satan attributes to God evil motives, when God only has our best interest at heart. Satan encourages Eve to doubt the goodness of God.

Men and women, when you and I face temptation, we come to that same conclusion. We think, "Is God really good in withholding this from me? Could He be better to me if He allowed this for me?"

Satan says, "Oh, God isn't as good to you as He could be, because He'd give you this if He were."

So, Satan doubts the goodness of God and attributes to God evil motives.

5. Satan promised blessings through disobedience

Look at the last part of verse 5.

. . . and you will be like God, knowing good and evil.

Satan says, "Sin will pay off. It'll bring dividends."

And it will, for a season. Make no mistake, however, where obedience to the words of Satan does offer benefits, they are only temporary. Obedience to the word of God offers benefits, but they are eternal.

That is the difference we find in Genesis 3. "Eat it," Satan says, "and you will be like your Creator; eat it, and you will be like God."

That is not happening today, is it? Yes, it is. In fact, the truth is, Satan is offering to mankind this very same thing. He is saying, "You are divine."

You might say, "I haven't heard that."

Genesis 3

Have you heard about channeling lately? It is sweeping America and is one of the arms of the New Age Movement. The New Age Movement is the repackaging of humanism. I think in its final form, it will literally win America. We will become like one of the eastern countries with all of its mysticism and many gods, unless God brings revival to America.

I was watching a talk show and on the program, a woman was channeling. If you are not aware of what that is, it is where some spirit from some other planet or some other universal life, inhabits the body of a human and speaks through them. That human becomes the channel through which the spirit speaks. This is not something new – it is as old as sin.

I was watching this particular talk show and the woman was channeling a spirit that had a strange Scottish type of accent. If I had been from Scotland, I think I would have been offended. Finally, someone from the audience raised the question, "Why did you come to planet Earth?"

Think about it, if you rule some universal planet out there, if you have your own kingdom, why take the time to come to Earth?

I will never forget the channeler's answer. Without even a blink of the eye, she said in that strange accent, "I have come to let man know that he is divine."

It is the lie of Satan. He says, "Man/woman, you are God."

Satan has transgressed the boundary between the Creator and the creature.

You say, "But I don't believe in channeling."

Let me ask a question of you. Would you espouse the words of one man who wrote the following that basically states the same thing? "Our responsibility is to direct our own lives, and we do not claim to be in need of forgiveness or salvation."

In other words, "I am the authority in my life. I run my life. I call the shots in my life."

What are you saying? That I am the God in my life; there is no other authority, no higher being. I live as if God does not exist. That is possible not only for an unbeliever, but for a believer as well.

Look at verse 6.

When the woman saw that the tree was good for food, . . .

(that is the physical lure),

. . . and that it was a delight to the eyes,

(that is the emotional lure),

. . . and that the tree was desirable to make one wise, . . .

(that is the intellectual lure),

. . . she took from its fruit and ate; and she gave also to her husband with her, and he ate.

Do you notice the three things? The emotional, the physical, and the intellectual lures? There will be times when it will make perfect sense to disobey God. There will be times in your life when it will just make common sense to do something other than what God declares. If you talk to someone who does not follow God, you will find that they always have their logic. God says that though it may make sense to you now, there is a coming judgment that ultimately brings death.

A Three-fold Discovery After Sinning

Now, I want to give a three-fold discovery after sinning.

1. They discovered their nakedness because of their sin

Look at the first part of Genesis 3:7.

Then the eyes of both of them were opened, and they knew that they were naked; . . .

The word "knew" in this verse, is the Hebrew word that could be translated, "they had intellectual insight". All of a sudden, they knew something was wrong.

2. They discovered self-effort

Look at the last part of verse 7.

. . . and they sewed fig leaves together and made themselves loin coverings.

This, ladies and gentlemen, is the first religious act of human history. This is the first act of self-effort to somehow cover over sin; to somehow make oneself better than you know you are. Adam, knowing that there is something wrong, something amiss, takes it into his own hands to remedy the situation.

My friend, let me suggest that if you do not know Jesus Christ as your personal Savior, you can come to church, but that is a fig leaf. You can pray prayers, but they are fig leaves. You can give money to church; you can give money away; you can attend a Bible study; you may even teach one, but they are all fig leaves. It is human self-effort to pull yourself up, to salve your conscience when you have never dealt with sin. That is what Adam and Eve did.

3. They discovered fear

Read the first phrase of Genesis 3:8.

They heard the sound of the Lord God . . .

That is not the sound of His voice, by the way, that is the literal sound of the Lord God walking. Evidently, He had taken some kind of human form or some kind of form that could make Him known to the senses of man. We do not know what kind of form that was. It may not have been a human form. Continue in verse 8,

They heard the sound of the Lord God walking in the garden in the cool of the day, and the man and the wife . . .

(notice what they did),

. . . hid themselves from the presence of the Lord God among the trees of the garden.

Adam and Eve discovered fear. Imagine, "Adam, I hear God. He's coming."

"Eve, I hear Him too. Let's run."

They run and hide behind some tree. There they are cowering and trembling in fear. Before the fall, they had perfect openness and communion with God. Now, they are hiding behind some shrub.

This is the nature of man. Because of sin, you and I do not run *to* God, we run *from* Him.

There is something beautiful, though, in the expression in the next verse, verse 9.

Then the Lord God called the man, and said to him, "Where are you?"

You run from Him, but, ladies and gentlemen, God has come to you; God has come to remedy the situation. And though you do not want Him, though you may not know Him, God in the person of Jesus Christ, who declared in the gospel of Luke (Luke 19:10), . . .

. . . [I am] come to seek and to save that which was lost.

. . . seeks after us. We would remain behind the shrub, if it were not for His grace.

The tragedy of this whole situation is that Adam and Eve, hiding behind the tree, thought they could get away from God. They thought that somehow God did not know. They are about to learn a lesson that you and I often forget. That is – God knows everything. They have not been clued in on that yet. They thought that they could hide behind the bark of a tree and get away from Him.

You and I often forget that God knows our sin, as well. We start at a very young age revealing the lack of understanding that God knows all. We try it out on our parents first. We did not need to have anyone teach that to us either.

I was sitting in the living room this past week, and one of my little boys walked in with the silliest grin on his face. Kids are so dumb! If he had done something wrong, he should have just acted normally, but he was giving me a silly little grin. And, he walks by me with his hands behind his back. His silly little grin got my attention, and then I noticed his hands were behind his back. Bright kid!

We are just as silly when we sin and give God some pious smile, as if He will not see; as if He will not know. Hebrews 4:13b, says,

. . . all things are open and laid bare to the eyes of Him . . .

A Four-fold Disintegration Resulting From Sin

I want to give a four-fold disintegration resulting from sin.

1. The disintegration of fellowship with God

Look at Genesis 3:9, 10.

Then the Lord God called the man, and said to him, "Where are you?" He said, "I heard the sound of You in the garden, and I was afraid because I was naked; . . .

(that is a lie),

". . . so I hid myself."

He should have said, "I heard the sound of You in the garden and I have sinned," but he said, "I was naked, so I hid myself."

Before the sin, there was openness and communication. Now, there is hiding in guilt.

2. The disintegration of marital unity

Continue to verses 11 and 12, and note this carefully.

And He said, "Who told you that you were naked? Have you eaten from the tree of which I commanded you not to eat?"

Boy, God is just like a parent, isn't He? Did you do what I told you not to do?

Adam has been called in on the carpet. There is no way out. So, what did he do? Verse 12 tells us.

The man said, "The woman whom You gave to be with me, she gave me from the tree, and I ate."

In other words, "Well, Lord, she, the one You gave me, she did it."

Now, use your imagination for a moment. We do not have it in the text, but I doubt Eve took that sitting down. I think the blood started going up in her neck; that little vein in her neck got ten times the normal size; her face flushed. She probably stomped her foot and said, "What?! What do you mean I made you do it? I can't make you do anything."

Adam said, "Well, you gave me the fruit."

They are having the first spat in marital history – and it is a "lulu".

Then she probably looked at the Lord and said, "Lord, I can't believe this man blames me." And God says, in verse 13a,

. . . What is this you have done? . . .

Now Eve is on the carpet. So she says, in the last part of the verse,

. . . The serpent deceived me, and I ate.

In other words, "Uh, the serpent, he made me do it."

Now Adam is hot. Oh boy. "What do you mean the serpent? You got on me because I blamed you, and now you're blaming the serpent."

Here they go. Yap! Yap! Yap! Yap! Yap! It is a good one.

How did they learn these techniques? Before this sin, they had never argued; they had perfect harmony. Now, at the drop of a hat, "bang," they are at each other's throats.

I will tell you why. It is because sin brought about a loss in marital harmony.

Three things were lost between husband and wife

Three things drastically changed and were lost between husband and wife.

A. Marriage lost its harmony

Adam and Eve blamed each other. I do not know where they learned the techniques of arguing, but they were masters at it all of a sudden.

I read of one newlywed couple who told some friends, "We decided we wouldn't go to sleep at night mad at one another. We haven't had any sleep for three weeks now."

That is so true. Why? Because it just comes naturally. What was unnatural in the garden; that is, arguing and a complaining spirit, is now natural.

B. Woman lost her naturally submissive spirit

Look at the first part of verse 16, which is a result of the sin or the fall. We will get back to verse 15 in a moment.

To the woman He said, "I will greatly multiply your pain in childbirth, in pain you will bring forth children; yet your desire will be for your husband . . .

Now the word "desire" could be translated, "crave". It is a pursuit. You could translate this phrase, "Your craving will be over your husband."

In other words, now because of the fall, it comes naturally for a woman to desire to form, manipulate, and move her husband. The reason that you, ladies, do that is because it is part of your nature now; because of sin. Her desire, that means her emotional being, is now exaggerated. Where once her husband was His, now she would seek to possess him. She now seeks to manipulate, to fashion, to form him after her own will.

C. Man lost his naturally loving headship

Notice the last part of verse 16.

. . . and he will rule over you.

The implication in this verse, of course, is the exaggerated sense that man will no longer lovingly lead. Now, man will tyrannically rule; will subjugate woman; will press her down.

In countries without the word of God, you will find women who are nothing more than beasts or objects. Even in America, where the word is not learned and loved, you will find women as objects, toys, beasts of burden.

Why? Why does man find it so easy to subjugate? Why does man find it so easy to tyrannically rule? It is because of sin. It now comes naturally to mankind to rule; to dominate without love.

3. The disintegration of man's paradise

Look at verse 17.

Then to Adam He said, "Because you have listened to the voice of your wife, and have eaten from the tree about which I commanded you, saying, 'You shall not eat from it'; cursed is the ground because of you; . . ."

In other words, what came naturally to the ground will be an unnatural thing. That is why when you plant tomatoes, what do you get? You get tomatoes and weeds. When you plant flowers, what do you get? You get flowers and weeds. Why? Because for every weed that grows, the earth is bearing witness that it is also under the curse. That which was unnatural is now natural.

Continue to the last part of verse 17.

. . . in toil you will eat of it all the days of your life.

Notice verse 18a,

Both thorns and thistles it shall grow for you; . . .

The Hebrew, in fact, could read, "Both thorns and thistles shall grow for you by themselves."

Look at verses 18b through 19a.

. . . and you will eat the plants of the field; by the sweat of your face you will eat bread . . .

I used to think that man would have to sweat to get bread, until I had the privilege of studying the original text. This literally means that man toils and he sweats, and interspersed between man sweating and toiling, he sits down to eat. In other words, work is broken up by his meals. Even when he sits down to eat, he is still sweating. Man is now cursed by being forced to plow an unyielding soil to work. Even in his eating, he does not rest.

4. The disintegration of physical immortality

Look at the last part of verse 19.

. . . Till you return to the ground, because from it you were taken; for you are dust, and to dust you shall return.

God's Four-fold Deliverance for Mankind

Let me give God's four-fold deliverance for mankind.

1. Victory is promised

Read verses 13 through 14.

Then the Lord God said to the woman, "What is this you have done?" And the woman said, "The serpent deceived me, and I ate." The Lord God said to the serpent, "Because you have done this, cursed are you more than all cattle, and more than every beast of the field; on your belly you will go, and dust you will eat all the days of your life;"

Now, however, notice the promise. This is called the "protoevangelium". It is the first promise of the gospel. Look at verse 15a.

And I will put enmity between you and the woman, and between your seed and her seed; . . .

There are two ways to interpret this, and I think both are correct. One is immediate and the other is prophetic.

The first interpretation is that the seed of the woman; that is, the woman following God, will be at enmity with the seed of the serpent. There is a clash, from this point until God reigns, between those who believe God and those who do not believe God. They will be at war.

Notice there is a prophetic utterance, as well. There is a change from the plural to the singular ("He," not "they"), in verse 15b,

. . . He shall bruise you on the head, and you shall bruise him on the heel.

Who is "He"? "He" is Jesus Christ.

Now, what does this verse mean when it says that the serpent will bruise His heel? I have been told and I would guess it to be true, although I never want to experience it, that if a serpent bites you, the best place to be bitten with the least results is the heel. In other words, what He is saying to the serpent is, "You're going to prick the coming Savior, but it will have no effect. And He will crush your head."

Now, if you want to kill a serpent, you do not cut off its tail. You do not crush a serpent's tail, you crush its head. This means that ultimately, he is brought to ruin. That is the promise of Jesus Christ.

Where would this take place? Where would the crushing occur? Where would the bruising of the heel take place? On the cross!! On the cross, the Savior's heel was pricked, but to no effect because He gained the victory over the grave. In that act He forever broke the power of sin that the serpent had over mankind. The promise is given.

2. Marital unity can be experienced

Look at the writings of Paul in Ephesians 5:18. He writes some unusual words in verse 18.

. . . do not get drunk with wine, . . . but be filled with the Spirit

This does not make a lot of sense unless you go back into history and understand the thinking of the Greeks. They taught in their mythology that their god Zeus, had a son one day. His son's name was Dionysius, and he was called the god of wine. In their religious system, the Greeks believed they must become drunk with wine. They would, of course, practice all kinds of perversion and filthiness and call it religion. In order to be able to practice such heinous crimes and sins against one another, they would become drunk to dull the senses and quiet the conscience.

This practice was evidently pervasive in the Ephesian society. So Paul comes along and says, "Now look, in worshipping God, don't become drunk with wine; don't be controlled by wine; don't be filled with that substance. Instead, be controlled by the spirit of God."

Guess what the first thing out of the bag is, as a result of being submissive to the Spirit of God? -- Wives submitting to husbands; husbands loving their wives. Marital unity can be experienced only if the power of Satan is quenched in the life of the believer in his practice by yielding to the Spirit of God.

3. Paradise will be re-established

This is a promise. Look at Revelation 21:1a.

Then I saw a new heaven . . .

(and guess what else),

. . . and a new earth . . .

Genesis 3

You and I think heaven is a floating cloud up there. It is also the re-establishment of paradise. Planet Earth is once again made like the days of creation for man to enjoy.

4. Physical immortality will be assured

Look at Revelation 22, and we will read some wonderful verses of scripture.

For all who believe in Jesus Christ (this is the promise), you are no longer under Satan's dominion, but are now serving the kingdom of God and His future coming kingdom.

Look at what it is going to be like, according to Revelation 22:1-5. Notice the reference with implications that go back to Genesis, chapter 3.

> *Then he showed me a river of water of life, clear as crystal, coming from the throne of God and of the Lamb, in the middle of its street. On either side of the river was the tree of life, . . .*

Now, at the end of Genesis, chapter 3, man is kept from the tree of life. However, once again, according to verse 2b, it is available,

> *. . . yielding its fruit every month; and the leaves of the tree were for the healing of the nations.*

Continue to verses 3 through 5.

> *There will no longer be any curse; and the throne of God and of the Lamb will be in it, and His bond-servants will serve Him; they will see His face, and His name will be on their foreheads. And there will no longer be any night; and they will not have need of the light of the lamp nor the light of the sun because the Lord God will illumine them; and they . . .*

(that is, the blood bought redeemed ones),

> *. . . will reign forever and ever.*

In Genesis 3, there is the curse, the fall, the expulsion, and "Goodbye to paradise." God closes the door on Eden. Revelation 22 promises the coming paradise; the coming kingdom. And those who believe in the Lamb will be able to participate in that coming kingdom.

Application –
Lessons to be Learned From the Fall!

Let me give three applications; three lessons that we can learn from the fall.

1. In the final analysis, sin never pays

Look at Genesis 3:23-24. Was it worth it for Adam and Eve to eat, to believe the lie of Satan?

Therefore, the Lord God sent him out from the garden of Eden, to cultivate the ground from which he was taken. So He drove the man out; and at the east of the garden of Eden He stationed the cherubim and the flaming sword which turned every direction to guard the way to the tree of life.

Literally, this does not mean there a sword that was on fire, but that there was a flame that was shaped like a sword, and it moved in every direction. That is as if it were lightning that flashed all around that tree as quickly as you could see. It is an awesome thing to think that there were cherubim, or angels, stationed around that tree, and a flashing of light all about it to keep man from coming near. It turned in every direction to guard the way to the tree of life.

2. Harmony in the home begins in the heart

Every Christian; every believer has the Holy Spirit dwelling within. To be controlled by the Holy Spirit is the key. It is that control that brings that harmonious state back to the home once again.

3. Paradise is designed for sinners – but those who have been forgiven

In a cemetery in Strasburgh, Pennsylvania, is the tomb of a soldier who died during the Civil War. Around that tombstone, of course, are many others. Abraham Lincoln sought to honor a soldier in a particular way. So, he chose one particular soldier's tombstone. Underneath his name and date of birth and death, Lincoln had written into the stone these words, "Abraham Lincoln's substitute." That soldier symbolized the fact that those who died in battle, died so others could live.

Men and women, you are either living under the curse of Genesis 3 or you have the promise of Revelation 22. What makes the difference is that you can look at the cross of Christ. You can think in your mind that Jesus Christ died one day for you, in your place, so that you can live. Can you put your name on the cross, "Stephen Davey's substitute"? If you cannot see your name; if you have never gone to the cross, you are under the curse. If you have gone to the cross, then paradise and abundant life, marital harmony, and forgiveness for sin will be once again experienced.

Goodbye to Paradise

Goodbye to Paradise

Genesis 3

Digging Deeper:

Everyday we need to be diligent and keep a watch for Satan's schemes. He is looking for any and every way to take our focus from God. When we least expect it, he is there.

> II Corinthians 2:11 *so that no advantage would be taken of us by Satan, for we are not ignorant of his schemes.*

1) If Satan takes advantage of us and takes our focus from God, even a little, what does Satan gain from this? What is his motivation?

_____

_____

_____

_____

2) As a believer, you will want to fellowship with other believers. You will find yourself drawn to others who trust in Jesus Christ. Why is this a good thing?

_____

_____

_____

> Ecclesiastes 4:9-12a *Two are better than one because they have a good return for their labor. For if either of them falls, the one will lift up his companion. But woe to the one who falls when there is not another to lift him up. Furthermore, if two lie down together they keep warm, but how can one be warm alone?*

Hold close to the word of God. Satan will take every opportunity to pull us away from God and His word. He will distort God's word,. He will try to trick us and seduce us. When we have the opportunity to sin, we can either believe the truth of God or the lies of Satan. God always tells the truth. In John 8:44b, Jesus declares,

> *. . . [Satan is] the father of lies.*

3) Satan is cunning. Can you see Satan's lies influencing your life? Give examples.

_____

_____

_____

_____

4) Find references in God's word that refute these lies.

_____

_____

_____

_____

_____

_____

Whose words are you going to follow?

How does Satan tempt us? He appeals to our appetite (physical), our emotion and our intellect/pride. Pride was part of Satan's own downfall. Satan's fall is described in Ezekiel. He wanted to be the most beautiful, better than God.

5) Compare Satan's character as described in Ezekiel with the temptation that he gives to Eve in Genesis 3:5

> *For God knows that in the day you eat from it, your eyes will be opened,. and you will be like God, knowing good and evil.*

_____

_____

_____

_____

How has pride penetrated your life? How are you looking to yourself, instead of to God?

The first gospel (protoevangelium) is given in Genesis 3:15.

> *And I will put enmity between you and the woman, and between your seed and her seed; He shall bruise you on the head, and you shall bruise him on the heel.*

This describes the fight between good and evil. This describes Satan and foretells the coming of Jesus Christ. There will be war between those that believe God and those that do not – between those that follow God and those that choose to follow Satan.

But, one day, Jesus Christ will come. Satan will move men to hang Him on a cross. Jesus will defeat death and thus defeat sin. Jesus will crush the serpent's head. That is the prophesy of Genesis 3:15.

6) Christ has given us a way to be forgiven of our sins. What is required of us to accept God's promise?

_____

_____

_____

Take It To Heart:

Through Adam's sin, all mankind is condemned, but because of Jesus' obedience, all sin can be forgiven.

Roman 5:19 *For as through the one man's disobedience the many were made sinners, even so through the obedience of the One the many will be made righteous.*

Once we had paradise. We had harmony. There was no fear, no jealousy, and no immorality. Then, through one man, Adam, sin entered the world. Through his seed, Adam has passed sin from generation to generation.

We will have paradise again one day. God has made this promise. God never lies.

Revelation 22:1-5 *Then he showed me a river of water of life, clear as crystal, coming from the throne of God and of the Lamb, in the middle of its street. On either side of the river was the tree of life, bearing twelve kinds of fruit, yielding its fruit every month; and the leaves of the tree were for the healing of the nations. There will no longer be any curse; and the throne of God and of the Lamb will be in it, and His bond-servants will serve Him; they will see His face, and His name will be on their foreheads. And there will no longer be any night; and they will not have need of the light of the lamp nor the light of the sun because the Lord God will illumine them; and they will reign forever and ever.*

So, my friends, we can listen to **Satan's deceptions** as he tries to pull us away from God. Or, we can listen to **God's truths** as he leads us to paradise.

"Which will you choose?"

The Curse of Cain

Genesis 4

Introduction

Today, we are going to discuss Genesis 4. It is a good illustration of sin because all men are sinners, all men are condemned, all men are without excuse. In this chapter, we will find depravity rearing its ugly head just outside the garden of Eden.

Genesis 4 provides the only authoritative account of early civilization. It is a little different of course, than scientists' accounts or anthropological writings that would suggest that early man was a cave man who walked around carrying a club and dragging his woman by the hair of her head. Such accounts are not exactly true.

As a matter of fact, early man was incredibly intelligent; they were geniuses. We will find in the ancestors of Cain, the first and second generation of Adam and Eve, that they were creating incredible things. They were inventing such things as musical instruments and metallurgy. They were inventing all kinds of things that would rapidly move a primitive society toward the kind of society that you and I enjoy in many ways today.

So, do not be fooled by society's accounts of early man. Early men were not dumb cave men, but were brilliant, as we will discover in this chapter.

Now, in the study of the life of Cain in Genesis 4, the first question I usually hear is, "Where did Cain get his wife?" Usually, that question comes from a person who does not want to talk about anything related to the gospel. They will say, "Where did Cain get his wife? Explain that to me and I will believe the rest of the Bible."

Let me answer that briefly, before we continue to the rest of Cain's biography. Cain married his sister. Before the law came, when God gave the genetic boundaries and the penalty for breaking the boundaries, men and women were married within the family.

It was the command of God to multiply and fill the earth. Obviously, Adam and Eve were the only parents. We know from Genesis 5:4-5, that Adam lived for nine hundred thirty years. Notice what happened during those hundreds of years – he had a lot of children. Look at verse 4.

Then the days of Adam after he became the father of Seth were eight hundred years, and he had other sons and daughters.

Adam multiplied his little corner of the earth. His quiver was full. So, Cain had quite a selection. He chose one of his sisters.

Why God Refused Cain's Offering

Now, the more important question is addressed in chapter 4. Let us begin with verse 1.

Now the man had relations with his wife Eve, and she conceived and gave birth to Cain, and she said, "I have gotten a manchild with the help of the Lord."

That is interesting because I believe that that is a simple statement of faith; that Eve is resting on the promise of God to bring a man, a seed, from her womb that would be the Savior. Of course, it is not Cain. Continue to verse 2.

Again she gave birth to his brother Abel. And Abel was a keeper of flocks, but Cain was a tiller of the ground.

Abel was the first herdsman or shepherd and Cain was the first farmer. Both of these occupations were worthy and ones that they chose.

Look at verses 3 through 5a.

So it came about in the course of time that Cain brought an offering to the Lord of the fruit of the ground. Abel, on his part also brought of the firstlings of his flock and of their fat portions. And the Lord had regard for Abel and his offering; but for Cain and for his offering, He had no regard. . . .

Let me answer one question, "Why did God refuse Cain's offering?" I will give three reasons.

1. Cain's offering was bloodless

In the New Testament in Hebrews 9:22, we read that there is no atoning or remission for sin apart from the shedding of blood.

Now, there are some views that I will not take the time to address, that suggest Cain came to God with a bad attitude and it was because of his attitude that God rejected his offering. I think the text would indicate otherwise.

- First, notice both Cain and Abel brought an offering.

That is not a coincidence. Verse 3 says,

So it came about in the course of time that Cain [and Abel] brought an offering to the Lord . . .

These terms are related to the giving of an offering. I think it is implied in this verse that Abel and Cain built an altar. On that altar, they placed their offerings. How did Cain know and learn that they were to bring an offering to God? This is an argument of course, without text, but I think God instructed them by their parents, Adam and Eve.

Let me give another reason why I believe Cain's offering was rejected because it was without blood.

- Secondly, they both came at an appointed time.

Notice again the phrase in verse 3, "in the course of time". What I am trying to do is prove that God gave Cain and Abel revelation about bringing sacrifices to God. The phrase "it came about in the course of time," could be literally translated, "at the end of days," which is a reference to the Sabbath day. These men brought their offerings on the seventh day. Was that coincidental? Absolutely not. It was a result of revelation.

- Thirdly, I think that revelation would be given in Genesis 3:21,

The Lord God made garments of skin for Adam and his wife, and clothed them.

As we studied earlier, Adam and Eve, in the garden, tried to cover their sin with fig leaves. That was not sufficient because that was the work of their hands. God kills some animals and takes the skins and clothes Adam and Eve. I think in that clothing, He gave them added revelation.

Genesis 4

There is only one way to atone for sin. Atonement, by the way, means covering. You cannot cover sin with the leaf of a tree. You must cover or atone for it by the shedding of blood; by the giving of another life. Fig leaves will never atone.

So, I think God refused Cain's offering because, first of all, it was bloodless.

2. Cain's offering was the fruit of his own hands

This is the religion of the world from the time of Cain; that is, we will approach God by the works of our hands; we will seek to satisfy a holy God by something that we do. That was insufficient because our own works can never atone for sin.

3. Cain's offering was the fruit of the ground

Cain ignored the curse. Look at a passage we studied earlier in Genesis 3:17.

Then to Adam He said, "Because you have listened to the voice of your wife, and have eaten from the tree about which I commanded you, saying, 'You shall not eat from it'; . . .

(note the curse),

"cursed is the ground because of you; in toil you will eat of it all the days of your life."

The earth had been cursed. There is nothing from this earth by the works of our hands that will ever satisfy a holy God. Cain tried. I think he rebelled against known revelation – revelation from God, in that they both brought an offering on the Sabbath day.

Now, notice what happens when God confronts Cain. Look at Genesis 4:5-6.

but for Cain and for his offering He had no regard. So Cain became very angry and his countenance fell. Then the Lord said to Cain, "Why are you angry? Why is your countenance fallen?"

It is almost as if God says, "Cain, you know what you're supposed to do. Why, now that you've disobeyed, are you angry with me?"

Notice what God says in verse 7a.

If you do well, . . .

(What would that be? Obviously God is saying, "If you do what I tell you to do."),

... will not your countenance be lifted up? And if you do not well, sin is crouching at the door; ...

The word "crouch" is used by the ancients to mean a lion that is crouching and ready to pounce on his prey. God is saying, "If you disregard My will, My revelation, My word, sin, like a lion, is crouching at your door ready to pounce. You are open prey."

Notice what He says in the next phrase of verse 7.

and its [sin's] desire is for you, ...

Does that ring a bell? Do you remember in Genesis 3:16, what God told the woman?

To the woman He said, "I will greatly multiply your pain in childbirth, in pain you will bring forth children; yet your desire will be for your husband ...

The same phrase that is used in this verse is used in referring to Cain's sin. In other words, "Your sin has the desire to control you."

Because of the fall, women try to control their husbands. That is part of the curse. It is part of sin that a woman now tries to manipulate and control her husband.

So, God is saying to Cain, "If you disregard My will, sin will manipulate you. Sin will control you, if you disregard My will."

The Five-fold Result of Cain's Sin

Now, notice the five-fold result of Cain's sin. By the way, Cain's sin was not murder; Cain's sin was disobedience. Murder is the first of five results of his sin. Five things happen because Cain disobeyed God's revelation.

Cain murdered his brother

Look at Genesis 4:8,

Cain told Abel, his brother. . . .

(What was he telling him? He was telling him about God. Perhaps he was arguing that God was playing favorites. We do not know.),

> *. . . And it came about when they were in the field, that Cain rose up against Abel his brother and killed him.*

Perhaps, if we could go back in time, we could watch two men out in the field. We cannot hear what they are saying, but we note that there is a heated argument going on. Cain is raising his fist to heaven. Abel is perhaps, pleading that he repent. Finally, Cain in his heated passion, picks up a blunt instrument or even takes his hands and beats Abel to death there in the field. He rose up and he killed him.

2. Cain lied to God

Look at verse 9a.

> *Then the Lord said to Cain, "Where is Abel your brother?"*

You may remember that when Adam sinned, God came and asked him a question. Well, in this verse, He is talking to the second generation and He asks a question and gives him a chance to repent. He says,

> *. . . "Where is Abel your brother?" . . .*

Note Cain's response in the next phrase of verse 9.

> *And he said, "I do not know." . . .*

That is a lie. Cain knows the exact spot where he has buried Abel so that no one will discover his sin. So he lies and says,

> *. . . "I don't know." . . .*

And then he asks the question in the last part of verse 9,

> *. . . "Am I my brother's keeper?"*

By the way, let me ask a question of you. What is the answer to that question? "Am I my brother's keeper?" Is the answer, "Yes," or "No"? The answer is "Yes," you are your brother's keeper. You do have a responsibility for your brother. Not only do we have responsibility for that family member, but of course, in the New Testament, in the body of Christ, you and I have a responsibility for one another as brothers and sisters in Christ.

Yes, I am my brother's keeper. There is a great sense that I am to know and I am to be concerned about where my brother is spiritually;

where his life is; where he resides in his relationship with God. Yes, I am my brother's keeper.

Then, in verse 10,

He [God] said, "What have you done? The voice of your brother's blood is crying to Me from the ground."

Cain murders his brother and then lies to God. Isn't that true of all of us? One of the first things to follow sin is a lie. Children lie to parents because they are living in sin. Parents lie to children to perhaps justify their sin. Husbands lie to wives, and wives lie to husbands. Why? Because there is sin at the door. To cover it, to clothe it, we begin telling one lie after another. Soon, it multiplies and becomes a tangled web, and we begin wondering, "What did I say?"

Someone said, "You never have to worry about what you said if you tell the truth."

So Cain began lying.

3. Cain lost his first love

Read on in verses 11 and 12a.

Now you are cursed from the ground, which has opened its mouth to receive your brother's blood from your hand. When you cultivate the ground, it will no longer yield its strengths to you; ...

Now, we can only understand this if we try to understand Cain. There is a breed of men called farmers, and they love the earth. Their greatest joy is watching the stalks of corn wave in the breeze. Nothing gives them more satisfaction than knowing that their barns are filled with fresh hay. They love the ground. It is their love, their life.

Cain chose the occupation of farmer because he loved the ground; he loved the earth. It was his greatest joy to plant seed and watch it grow and multiply. He brought to God the best things his hands had produced by his labor. He loved it, and God took it away from him. In effect, God said, "Cain, the earth is cursed, but now, the earth is going to ignore your hand. That means, Cain, that you're going to go out there and plant seed, and nothing is going to happen."

That would be the nightmare of a farmer. I can imagine that Cain probably went out immediately to test this. He probably planted some seed and watered it and watched over it for a few months. He perhaps, knelt and tried to coax it out of the ground, watering the ground with his tears, saying, "Please grow."

Yet, the curse stood true. The earth ignored Cain, a man who loved it so much. This was a result of the tragedy of sin.

4. Cain lost his sense of permanence and direction

Look at the last part of verse 12.

. . . you will be a vagrant and a wanderer on the earth.

In other words, "You are going to leave this place and spend the rest of your life wandering around."

Again, we cannot understand this unless we think in terms of what a farmer is like. Most farmers are born, grow up, live and die in the same town.

I was born in Worthington, Minnesota, just next to Butterfield, Minnesota. It is a farming community. I have not been back in ten years. We used to go back every summer, and I can still remember in my mind's eye, that little main street and the general store that was run for many decades by my aunt and uncle. All of the people in town knew each other. They were people of the earth; they farmed. In fact, my father was raised in a farmer's home, and he sold his inheritance and joined the Air Force and moved to the city. That is how I was raised in the city.

There in the little towns of Worthington and Butterfield, life is so simple. The farmers live close to the ground, and the roots are deep. They have lived there all their lives. There is a real sense of permanence. Nothing exciting in our definition, ever happens. In fact, their version of a crime wave would be some teenagers riding through town at eleven o'clock at night on their motorcycles or something. Nothing really flamboyant ever occurs. It is simply – you get up, you farm, you eat, you go to bed. And yet, they love it that way. You could not pull them into the city if you tried.

Think in terms of that when you think of Cain. Perhaps you have read or heard about all of the farmers over the last decade that have lost their farms. Unless you have been raised on a farm, you will never understand the agony of their hearts. To auction off what has been in the family for decades, generations, years – this is their life; their roots!

They live in the same home where grandpa and grandma lived, and now, they are losing it.

That is the way Cain felt. That is the tragedy of sin. Because God would virtually tell Cain, "Yank up all the roots. From now on, you wander. No more permanence; no more stability."

5. Cain lost his fellowship with God

Look at verses 13 through 15.

Cain said to the Lord, "My punishment is too great to bear! Behold, You have driven me this day from the face of the ground; and from Your face I will be hidden, and I will be a vagrant and a wanderer on the earth, and whoever finds me will kill me. So the Lord said to him. "Therefore whoever kills Cain, vengeance will be taken on him sevenfold." And the Lord appointed a sign for Cain, so that no one finding him would slay him.

This sign was not a mark, but a sign for Cain. We do not know what it was, but it was something that when others saw it, they knew they were not to touch Cain.

Cain was to live under the curse for his entire life. Continue to verse 16 and notice the first phrase.

Then Cain went out from the presence of the Lord, and settled in the land of Nod, east of Eden.

"Nod" is the Hebrew word which means, "the land of wandering". Cain would wander the rest of his life.

It is interesting that Cain rebelled against the curse because the text tells us, in verse 17, that he tried to build the city to gain some kind of permanence. The Hebrew text indicates there is not a completion of the work. In other words, he began to build, but he never finished. His children probably finished for him.

Cain continued wandering – a fugitive from God. There was no sign of repentance; no sign of confession. You never hear Cain say, "Okay, Lord, just a second. I'll go and get a lamb and be right back."

No. Cain took his basket of fruit, and we have every indication that he walked away from God forever.

We are told in Genesis 4:18-26, of his family.

Now to Enoch was born Irad, and Irad became the father of Mehujael, and Mehujael became the father of Methushael, and Methushael became the father of Lamech.

Lamech took to himself two wives: the name of one was Adah, and the name of the other, Zillah.

Adah gave birth to Jabal; he was the father of those who dwell in tents and have livestock.

(this guy invented the tent),

His brother's name was Jubal; he was the father of all those who play the lyre and the pipe.

As for Zillah, she also gave birth to Tubal-cain, the forger of all implements of bronze and iron; and the sister of Tubal-cain was Naamah.

(notice that it did not take millions of years for people to discover how to use iron and bronze),

Lamech said to his wives . . .

(in his proud heart),

"Adah and Zillah, listen to my voice, you wives of Lamech, give heed to my speech, for I have killed a man for wounding me; and a boy for striking me;

"if Cain is avenged sevenfold, then Lamech seventy-sevenfold."

(in other words, "I am more wicked than my father, and I am proud of it."),

Adam had relations with his wife again; and she gave birth to a son, and named him Seth, for, she said, "God has appointed me another offspring in place of Abel, for Cain killed him."

To Seth, to him also a son was born; and he called his name Enosh. Then men began to call upon the name of the Lord.

Application –
Two Thoughts From the Life of Cain

Let me give two thoughts from the life, the biography of Cain. It is brief, yet it is painful. The man who rejected the revelation of God took his own approach to God in his own hands and said, "I'll come to You, God, in my way." Like those today, who say they will approach God their way, God rejects them.

1. Disobedience to God never makes sense

The price of disobedience to God is too great. The penalty is more severe than any enjoyment you or I could ever receive from sin. Disobeying God never, ever makes sense.

I can remember, as I was growing up, listening to my father at the Friday night Bible study for military men. He would ask the question, and I used to chuckle because I knew what was coming, "Men, give me three logical reasons why you sin."

The guys would pop up their hands and say things like, "The devil made me do it."

They would give all the excuses. Then, my father would prove to them that there is no logical reason, no sensible reason why you or I would ever disobey God. Disobedience never, ever makes sense.

2. Obedience to God begins with a choice

Notice, although I have not spent any time on this and it is probably a sermon in itself, both Cain and Abel were born into the same home. Both boys had the same advantages and had the same amount of revelation from God. However, they proved to us that obedience is dependent upon choice.

One chose to follow the revelation of God, while the other chose to disobey the revelation of God. One came with humility, while the other came with pride. One came the way God commanded, while the other came his own way.

Let me close with a story that I love. Charlotte Elliott was a very troubled young lady. She was not a Christian, and in fact, was rebelling against what she knew to be true.

Charlotte was raised in a godly home. Her parents, out of desperation one evening, invited a visiting preacher into their home for dinner. He came in and began talking about the Lord at the table. They were asking questions for him to answer that would perhaps, probe into the heart of their daughter so that she would come to Christ.

Finally, she blew up and, in a rage, stomped off. They finished their meal in silence.

After awhile, Charlotte, sorry for her outburst, came back to the table. The family had been dismissed and only the preacher was there. He began urging her to choose Christ. She was so overwhelmed with all of her pride, with all of her sense of worth, that it took some talking to reveal to her that she was in fact, a sinner. She finally, after an hour or two of discussion, broke down.

Then, the greatest obstacle to Charlotte's mind and heart was the fact that she was too sinful for God to ever accept her. She was too filled with herself, her own works. The pastor began saying, "Charlotte, you've got to come to God just like you are. Come to God just like you are."

Still, the light did not break. The preacher left.

Charlotte stayed up all night with those words ringing in her mind, until finally, the Spirit of God made it clear. Her own testimony is written in a way that we sing. Let me read the words that Charlotte Elliott wrote.

Just as I am, without one plea,
But that Thy blood was shed for me,
And that Thou bidst me come to thee,
O Lamb of God, I come, I come.

Just as I am, and waiting not
To rid my soul of one dark blot,
To Thee whose blood can cleanse each spot,
O Lamb of God, I come, I come.

Just as I am, though tossed about
With many a conflict, many a doubt,
Fightings and fears within, without,
O Lamb of God, I come, I come.

Just as I am, Thou wilt receive,

Wilt welcome, pardon, cleanse, relieve;

Because Thy promise I believe,

O Lamb of God, I come, I come.

The hope for our lives, men and women, is the hope that Abel found in coming to God in His way, just as he was – a sinner. We have found the acceptance of one, due to obedience and the rejection of another because he came in the way that he wanted.

Oh, what a delight to know that, when I come to God by the way of the cross, just as I am (and Jesus continually accepts us on that same basis, just as we are), we can rest, just as we are, in Christ, forgiven, pardoned, and relieved. What a relief that is.

The Curse of Cain

Genesis 4

Digging Deeper:

Typically the best method for instructing someone is the simplest method. If you have children, many times you need to simplify the instructions. You will need to tell the child exactly what you want for them to do. God does this in Genesis 4. The instruction he gives to Cain is so simple and understandable, and at the same time, He tells Cain the simple and exact truth.

> Genesis 4:7 *If you do well, will not your countenance be lifted up? And if you do not well, sin is crouching at the door; and its [sin's] desire is for you, . . .*

Pretty simple....Do God's will and you'll be fine....Don't do God's will and sin will be waiting for you.

Again, God is telling us to keep our focus on Him, otherwise Satan will be there ready to pounce.

1) How have you kept your focus on God in the last 24 hours?

_____

_____

_____

2) Did you feel Satan tempt you? Trying to move your focus from God? How?

_____

_____

_____

God is so patient with us. We sin and he gives us a chance to repent. God really wants us to be close to Him.

Luke (Luke 19:10), . . .*[I am] come to seek and to save that which was lost.*

Adam sinned in the Garden. God came to Adam and gave him a chance to repent. But Adam tried to hide from God. He tried to hide his sin from God. Now, in Chapter 4, Cain is going to lie to God and try to hide his sin.

Genesis 4:9 *Then the Lord said to Cain, "Where is Abel your brother?" And he said, "I do not know."* . . .

When will we learn that we can not hide our sin from God? He knows everything. We are fallen man and thus, we will sin. God knows this, but through His grace, He has given us a chance to repent.

Are you taking advantage of God's grace?

What sin are you trying to hide from God? -- Some little white lie, "surely God would not know about that..."   Do you see Satan *crouching,* waiting to *pounce....*

We that are the body of the church of Christ are all brothers and sisters in Christ. We should protect our brothers and sisters from Satan. We are "our brother's keeper."

3) Describe what it means to be "your brother's keeper."

_____

_____

_____

_____

Sin has many consequences. Cain had several terrible results from his sin. He murdered his brother, he lied to God and he lost his ability to be a farmer. But central to all of these results, Cain lost his fellowship with God. It is interesting to see the picture of Cain.

117

He becomes a wanderer. He becomes a person with no direction. This is a very true and accurate picture of a person that has lost fellowship with God. Cain searched for things to take God's place. He searched for permanence. When we stray from God, what are we searching for? God is all we need. But, sometimes we search for more.

4) Review the last week in your life. .Name 5 things or situations that have tempted you to stray from God?

_____

_____

_____

_____

_____

When you pray, do you ask God to remove the temptations from your path? You should add something to that prayer. Ask God to give you the strength to want to avoid and ignore temptation. These temptations will always exist for us. You should pray for the desire to strengthen your fellowship with God and the desire to recognize and avoid temptations.

5) When you are in a right relationship with God, how should you handle the above 5 temptations?

_____

_____

_____

_____

_____

_____

Take It To Heart :

We never see Cain come back to God and repent. Cain was a sinner, just as we are sinners. Cain lost his fellowship to God and wandered the rest of his life trying to find something or someone to take God's place. Look around you, in your workplace, maybe even in your family. You will see people looking for a substitute for God. Nothing can ever take God's place. Nobody can ever fulfill your life like God can.

What do you see others using as a "substitute" for God?

How will these "substitutes" fulfill their needs?

How will these "substitutes" take them down a "road" away from God?

Truths From an Ancient Record

Genesis 5

Introduction

If you have decided to read through the Bible from cover to cover, and you have started in the book of Genesis, the first major hurdle you have had to overcome is Genesis 5. In fact, many people have never hurdled it and have stopped in their reading at that point.

In one sense Genesis 5, seems unimportant to the twentieth century Christian. In another sense it seems almost discouraging or despondent. In this chapter, you are walking through a cemetery viewing the headstones of the deceased patriarchs.

Why would God spend time recording this ancient obituary column for us in Genesis, chapter 5? I must admit or confess that those thoughts have crossed my mind. In fact, I considered skipping chapter 5 with only a few comments, and then getting into the more exciting chapter 6 of Genesis. We know the story of Noah and the flood.

However, as I plowed into Genesis 5, it was not long before I discovered many precious gems. In fact, when I finished the week of study, I even entertained the thought of making this a two or three part sermon. We will never get through Genesis that way, right? And all of you want to get through Genesis eventually. So, we will cover some of the key thoughts in Genesis, chapter 5.

Why Did God Record an Obituary Column?

Let us answer the first question. I will give three answers to the question, "Why would God take the time to record this chapter of the generation of Adam? Why did God record an obituary column?"

Let us begin by looking at Genesis 5:1-3a.

This is the book of the generations of Adam. In the day when God created man, He made him in the likeness of God. He created them male and female, and He blessed them and named them Man in the day when they were created. When Adam had lived one hundred and thirty years, he became the father . . .

Genesis 5

Now we begin making our way through the graveyard. Why take the time to give us this? Let me give three suggestions.

1. God is implying first, that He is keeping His word.

God had promised a deliverer through the godly seed of woman. He is listing the names of those in the godly line of Seth. Chapter 4 of Genesis lists the ungodly line of Cain. God is taking time to remind Israel that, "I have kept a godly seed alive through Seth, and here are their names."

2. The second implication is that God always has a remnant of believers.

The God-fearing may be a tiny minority. In fact, at the writing of this, man was becoming increasingly immoral. Yet God is letting us in on the fact that there are those who have not "thrown in the towel"; there are still some who follow God.

I think of Elijah, who, when he took on the prophets of Baal, won the great victory on Mount Carmel. The fire fell and he was on the mountaintop experience of victory. Then he had all of the false prophets rounded up and they were all killed. He had also been praying for three years that no rain would come, and it had not. God had answered his prayer as the prophet.

However, after Mount Carmel, Jezebel says these words in I Kings 19:2b,

... So may the gods do to me and even more, if I do not make your life as the life of one of them [prophets of Baal] by tomorrow about this time.

In other words, she is saying, "You've got twenty-four hours to live, and then it's curtains; you're done. I've put a contract out on your head, and I'm going to make sure this time tomorrow, you're dead."

You may remember the story that Elijah runs for his life. He is tired and discouraged. This is what he prays to God, in I Kings 19:4b, 10. Have you ever prayed this?

It is enough; now, O Lord, take my life, for I am not better than my fathers. . . . I have been very zealous for the Lord, the God of hosts; for the sons of Israel have forsaken Your covenant, torn down Your altars and killed Your prophets with the sword. . . .

(note this),

. . . And I alone am left; and they seek my life, to take it away.

God, I think, chuckles under His breath and then, moves closer to Elijah and whispers in his ear these words, "Son, there are seven thousand people in Israel alone who have never bowed their knee to Baal. Seven thousand – unknown, unnamed – believers in Me. You don't know who they are; you don't know where they are, but I want you to know that I have a remnant. And they have never bowed their knee to the false gods." (I Kings 19:18)

I think of what Paul wrote to the Philippians 4:22. He said these words,

All the saints greet you, especially those of Caesar's household.

We are never given their names, but in the ungodly household of this emperor lived a believing remnant – those who were following God.

And how about that long list of names in Romans, chapter 16? There are names like Aristobulus, and Junias, and Phlegon, and others that we have never even heard of. They were unnoticed and unnamed, but they were not forgotten. They might have been in the minority, but they were never overwhelmed.

Let me apply this thought to you. Perhaps this past week, you have had the thought that you are alone in your walk with the Lord – but you are not. You might even find yourself in the minority in your family. When Thanksgiving and Christmas family reunions come along, the last thing they do is lighten your load; refresh your heart. Instead, they increase the burden of your heart. You are the tiny minority in that realm of relatives that you see every year or every other year. You might be in the minority at your job, where it seems that you are the only one that has not bowed his knee to the gods of materialism and pleasure. So, you get to the point where you bow your knee to the Lord, and say, "Lord, this isn't worth it. I am the only one."

I want you to hear today, my friend, from Genesis, chapter 5, God whispering in your ear, "Son [or daughter], you are not alone. I have a godly remnant out there – thousands here, hundreds there, one or two tucked away over there that you do not know about. You're not alone."

3. The third implication is that God never forgets His own people.

Now, chapters 1 through 11 in the book of Genesis cover two thousand years. There are two thousand years to cover in eleven chapters. Do you know what you and I would have done? For heaven sake, we would never have taken an entire chapter to list peoples' names. There is too much to cover; too much ground in the history of the world. He has two thousand years to cover and He stops to give us a list of names.

It is interesting that God is particularly concerned to record the names of those who follow Him. One illustration would be Malachi in Genesis 3:16, where the prophet writes,

Then those who feared the Lord spoke to one another, and the Lord gave attention and heard it, and a book of remembrance was written before Him for those who fear the Lord and who esteem His name.

Revelation 20:11-15, tell us that the names of those who believe in the Lamb are written in the book of life. Isn't it an interesting thought, ladies and gentlemen, that God is interested in you? He is so interested that He has recorded your name. You and I have a hard time remembering names, but God never forgets. If you believe in Him, He will never forget you.

Do you know what it is like to be forgotten? Perhaps some husband this past week, forgot a birthday and is in trouble today. Or perhaps you forgot an anniversary – that is worse.

I grew up in a rather large family of four boys and our parents. In the afternoons, my father, my brothers and I would frequently play basketball at the public school. One day, when my youngest brother was about four years old, we were at the school playing. We played and had a great time and then, piled back into the car and headed home. About ten blocks down the street, someone asked, "Hey, where's Jonathan?"

We had forgotten the poor kid! So, we turned around and went back, and there was Jonathan walking down the street with his hands tucked in his pockets. He looked so forlorn; so forgotten. I can remember my father trying to explain to him, "I love you, son, I just forgot you."

Perhaps you know what it is like to be forgotten at the airport. Someone did not come and pick you up – they forgot.

It is easy for us to forget, but God never does. He is letting us know in Genesis, chapter 5, that, "I remember all those who believe in My name."

Two Notable Mentions

Now that we have discovered a few general principles, let us look at some specifics. We will not take the time to study all who are mentioned in Genesis 5. There are two men of notable mention in this long list. These men are kind of the salutatorians of the graduating class of patriarchs. The two men are Enoch and Methuselah. Since God took special time with them, let us spend some time with them as well.

Enoch

Four phrases about Enoch

Enoch appears five times in Scripture and four different phrases or thoughts are connected with this man. Let me give them to you.

1. Enoch was the seventh generation from Adam

Turn to Jude, the small book with only one chapter that is just before Revelation, the last book of the Bible. Jude, verse 14, says,

. . . Enoch, in the seventh generation from Adam . . .

Why is this mentioned? If you go back to Genesis 4:17, you discover that in the line of Cain, there is an Enoch. There are two Enochs that are contemporaries living at the same time. God is saying, "I want you to know about the godly Enoch, the one who followed Me, not the one in the line of Cain. This Enoch, in the line of Seth, is the seventh generation from Adam. He is the godly one."

That gives us an illustration that during the course of world history, there will be the Enochs who follow God and the Enochs who follow the way of Cain.

2. The second thing that is said about Enoch is that he was a preacher of righteousness.

Look again at Jude, verses 14 through 15.

It was also about these men that Enoch, in the seventh generation from Adam, prophesied, saying, "Behold the Lord came with many thousands of His holy ones, to execute judgment upon all, and to convict all the ungodly of all their ungodly deeds which they have done in an ungodly way, and of all the harsh things which ungodly sinners have spoken against Him."

You should underline the word "ungodly," as it appears four times in these two verses.

Enoch was a preacher, and his sermons were two-fold, or had two themes: the current ungodliness and the coming judgment. Boy, Enoch was a popular preacher – he preached about those things. Enoch's preaching on the subject of ungodliness was so well known that within his autobiographical statement, he used the word "ungodly" four times.

The interesting thing is, who his audience was – they were his relatives; those related to him. He did not have an easy task, and yet he preached righteousness.

3. Enoch walked with God   (Genesis 5:22a).

Then Enoch walked with God three hundred years . . .

This was not just for a day, a week, a year – no, Enoch walked with God three hundred years.

The original stem of the word "walk" would indicate close and intimate communion. Enoch enjoyed fellowship with God. Notice this is a walk, not a hundred yard sprint. It is not a mad dash, but a walk. It is also not a casual "take it or leave it" stroll. No, this in an intimate walk; this is a pursuit.

Two things necessary for a walk with God

This is a subject for an entire sermon, but let me at least suggest two things that are necessary for you to walk with God.

Harmony

You cannot take a walk with someone you are at odds with, there must be harmony. A walk with someone in an intimate fellowship means that your hearts are in harmony.

Agreement

You are agreeing, as Enoch did, with the direction God is going. I think the reason more of us do not want to walk consistently with God is because of the times in our lives when we do not like the direction He is taking us. We say, "turn left"; He says, "turn right". We say, "stop"; He says, "continue". So we say, "Well, Lord, I don't like the direction of this walk. I can't agree."

For three hundred years, Enoch obviously agreed.

4. Enoch walked by faith

The fourth descriptive thought concerning Enoch is found in Hebrews 11:5. I believe this is even more powerful an implication that his walk. It is obviously a synonymous thought and yet it is distinct. Enoch was taken up so that he would not see death.

> *By faith . . .*

(that was the key),

> *. . . Enoch was taken up so that he would not see death; and he was not found because God took him up; for he obtained the witness that before his being taken up he was pleasing to God.*

Note that Enoch's reputation before his being taken up was that he was pleasing to God. Enoch pleased God.

You might think, "Well that's great for Enoch. He was a great man of the faith. He was one of the patriarchs. He had an extra dose of grace. I mean, God kind of padded the way for him. He could please God. Is it really up to me to please God today?"

Well, there are several times in the New Testament that the word "ambition" is used. One of these texts is in II Corinthians 5:9 where Paul says,

> *. . . we also have as our ambition, whether at home or absent, to be pleasing to Him [God].*

We are ambitious to please God.

How do we please God? This again is a subject for another study, but let me point out one thought. Turn to I Kings 3. I want to take you to an incident in Scripture where a man did something and then, we hear God saying, "Hey, that pleased me."

I think we can learn what it takes to please God from this one incident. Look at I Kings 3:5,

> *In Gibeon the Lord appeared to Solomon in a dream at night; and God said, "Ask what you wish Me to give you."*

How would you like that for Christmas? Anything you want – you wish for it, you have got it. Boy, I can think of three or four things, right away!

So, in verse 6,

> *Then Solomon said, "You have shown great lovingkindness to Your servant David my father, according as he walked before You in truth and righteousness and uprightness of heart toward You; and You have reserved for him this great lovingkindness, that You have given him a son to sit on his throne, as it is this day."*

Well, get to the wish, Solomon. Continue to I Kings 3:7 ,8.

> *Now, O Lord my God, You have made Your servant king in place of my father David, yet I am but a little child; I do not know how to go out or come in. Your servant is in the midst of Your people which You have chosen, a great people who are too many to be numbered or counted.*

In verse 9 is Solomon's wish.

> *So give Your servant an understanding heart to judge Your people to discern between good and evil. For who is able to judge this great people of Yours?*

Continue to verse 10.

> *It was pleasing in the sight of the Lord that Solomon had asked this thing.*

Now, in the next verse, God will put His spell out the three wishes that you and I would normally ask. Look at verse 11.

> *God said to him, "Because you have asked this thing and have not asked for yourself long life, . . .*

(that is the first thing – health),

. . . nor have asked riches for yourself, . . .

(that is the second thing – wealth),

. . . nor have you asked for the life of your enemies, . . .

(that is the third thing – no enemies; popularity),

. . . but have asked for yourself discernment to understand justice,

Health, wealth, and fame – those are the three wishes that we would have made. God said, "Because you didn't ask for these three, but instead asked for discernment to understand justice," – continue to verse 12a,

behold, I have done according to your words. . . .

What pleases God, ladies and gentlemen, from this little incident? It is when you and I pray, "Lord, I don't ask for help, I just ask for the discernment to understand when sickness comes. Lord, I'm not going to ask or wish for wealth, I just ask for the prudence and the wisdom to steward what you have given me. Lord, I don't ask for popularity or fame, I just ask for grace to handle my enemies."

Then, God says to you and me, "I'm pleased."

Methuselah

Note one other honorable mention in Genesis, chapter 5. God mentions another man, just briefly, and yet there is so much about this one character. Methuselah is the second honorable mention in verse 22.

> *Then Enoch walked with God three hundred years after he became the father of Methuselah, and he had other sons and daughters.*

Three thoughts about Methuselah

1. First, Methuselah's birth evidently brought about a change in his father's life.

Look at verse 22 again, and note the word "after".

Then Enoch walked with God three hundred years <u>after</u> he became the father of Methuselah . . .

129

The cry of his newborn son pierced Enoch's heart. God used that to cause the understanding and desire in his heart that, "Now my son is watching. He is here and I must now walk with God."

For three hundred years after Methuselah's birth, Enoch followed God and pleased God.

There is a story of the alcoholic who lived a terrible life of sin. He abused his wife, never took care of things around the home, and spent most of his money on liquor. Into their home a baby boy was born, and the entire town thought it was a tragedy for a baby boy to be born into a home like that. And indeed, this man continued his carousing and drinking, never giving any thought to his son and wife.

One winter, however, when the boy was five, the father slammed out of the house and began walking across the freshly driven snow toward the local tavern. As he was walking, he heard the door close behind him and someone call out, "Daddy, slow down."

The father turned around and found his son taking large strides so he could step where his father had already pressed the snow down. His father angrily said, "Son, get back in the house. What are you doing?"

The son stopped and kind of stuck out his chest and said, "Daddy, I'm big enough now, so that wherever you step, I can step. Now I can follow in your footsteps."

That man turned and came back to his son, and he knelt in the snow, gathered his boy into his arms, and said to his son, "In that case, I need to change directions."

Now we do not know what Enoch was like before the birth of his son. However, something about his birth told Enoch, "Even though you're in the godly line, you have not been godly and you need to change direction; you need to begin walking with God."

The best thing that you and I can do for our children, men and women, is not provide for them the most expensive education, not give them the finest clothes and automobiles. The best thing that we can do for our children is to walk with God. We need to press down the ground where we are not ashamed if they should follow step after step.

2. The second thing about Methuselah's name is the meaning of his name. The name means "when he is dead, it will come".

That is a great name to have. Names were always chosen according to meaning, so Enoch saw his baby boy and thought, "What should I name this boy so that the meaning will ring into the ears of all who hear it? Methuselah means, 'when he is dead, it will come'."

That is a strange name, unless you understand the chronological history. History reveals that the year Methuselah died, the flood covered the earth. Now, according to Jude, verse 14, Enoch was a prophet. God must have given him revelation that when his little boy died – and he would not know if that would be in two weeks, two years, two hundred years – but when Methuselah died, it would come, meaning the judgment.

3. Methuselah lived longer than any other person ever lived.

Do you get this? God said, "When this boy dies, judgment is coming."

However, in order to illustrate His grace and patience towards humanity, he made it so that Methuselah would live longer than anyone ever lived. When Methuselah died, judgment came.

"And He Died"

One phrase receives repeated attention in Genesis, chapter 5. It is the phrase, "and he died".

In:

- verse 5 – *So all the days that Adam lived were nine hundred and thirty years, <u>and he died</u>.*

- verse 8 – *So all the days of Seth were nine hundred and twelve years, <u>and he died</u>.*

- verse 11 – *So all the days of Enosh were nine hundred and five years, <u>and he died</u>.*

- verse 14 – *So all the days of Kenan were nine hundred and ten years, <u>and he died</u>.*

- verse 17 – *So all the days of Mahalalel were eight hundred and ninety-five years, <u>and he died</u>.*

- verse 20 – *So all the days of Jared were nine hundred and sixty-two years, <u>and he</u> <u>died.</u>*
- verse 27 – *So all the days of Methuselah were nine hundred and sixty-nine years, <u>and he died.</u>*
- verse 31 – *So all the days of Lamech were seven hundred and seventy-seven years, <u>and he died.</u>*

Lamech, the last in this genealogical record, lived seven hundred and seventy-seven years and guess what happened? And he died.

God told Adam, in Genesis 2:17b,

. . . in the day that you eat from it [the tree of the knowledge of good and evil] you will surely die.

In Genesis 5:5 we are told,

So all the days that Adam lived were nine hundred and thirty years, and he died.

God kept His word. And, by the way, ladies and gentlemen, that is why one day, you and I will grace the column of some obituary in the newspaper. We, like Adam, will die. We cannot avoid it, except for the coming of Jesus Christ for the church.

There is a fable of a wealthy merchant who sent his servant to the market in Samaria to purchase goods that were needed. The servant went to the market in obedience to his master and began making purchases. He then decided to take a little shortcut through an alley. Halfway there, he ran face to face with lady death. The fable tells that this servant was so startled that he turned and ran. Lady death must be after him! He ran back to his master and said, "Please loan me one of your fastest horses. I must flee to Baghdad tonight."

The master could tell his servant was distraught. He said, "Okay, take the horse, it's yours."

So, the servant fled to Baghdad. The master then went to the market in Samara and finished buying the needed goods. He also went back through the alley, and came face to face with lady death. He, perhaps knowing that his time had not come, said to lady death, "Why have you startled my servant?"

Lady death said to him, "Actually it was I who was startled. I couldn't understand why he was in Samaria. I have an appointment with him tonight in Baghdad."

The writer of Scripture tells us in Hebrews 9:27,

. . . it is appointed for men to die once . . .

That could be literally translated, "It is the destiny of everyone to die."

We do not like to think about that. And yet, one of the godliest men who ever lived said, in Psalm 90:12a,

[Lord] teach us to number our days . . .

We are not ready to live, until we are prepared to die.

Truths From an Ancient Record

Genesis 5

Digging Deeper:

Do you ever feel alone as a Christian? At work, at home, or at a social event? Around you are unbelievers. Do you stand out as a Christian? By the way, this is a great compliment. I want my faith to be **strong** enough so that I can **stand out as a Christian.** We need to be different than the "crowd." One who follows God will walk a narrow road.

> Matthew 7:13 *Enter through the narrow gate; for the gate is wide and the way is broad that leads to destruction, and there are many who enter through it.*

God gave us Genesis 5 for many reasons. One of those is to remind us that we are **NOT** alone. He will put believers around us that will encourage us at just the right time. Even in the darkest times and even when we feel the most vulnerable, God will put somebody there to help us stay focused on God.

1) Describe a situation in your life where you feel the most alone in your walk with God. Describe what you "draw on" to keep your focus on God in this situation.

_____

_____

_____

_____

_____

_____

> Genesis 5:22a **Then Enoch walked with God three hundred years ...**

Enoch walked with God for 300 years. To consistently walk with God Enoch must have had a great **focus** on God. There must have been many times he could have wavered. To be this strong, Enoch must have had God in his heart and in his mind. Moses described this kind of faith in his exhortation to the Israelites.

> Deuteronomy 6:5 **You shall love the LORD your God with all your heart and with all your soul and with all your might.**

2) Explain how "harmony" and "agreement" are essential for our strong walk with God.

_____

_____

_____

_____

_____

Enoch pleased God. We, also, should be pleasing to God. But how do we know if we are pleasing God? Paul gives us a good starting point in his letter to the Corinthians.

> II Corinthians 5:9 . . . **we also have as our ambition, whether at home or absent, to be pleasing to Him [God].**

The Greek word for "ambition" denotes to strive earnestly and to make it one's aim. The only way we will be pleasing to God is if we take aim at that goal and strive with all our might.

135

Methuselah lived longer than any other person ever lived. He lived for 969 years before he died. His father, Enoch, was a profit and in what must have been a prophetic revelation named his son Methuselah, which in Hebrew means, "when he is dead, it will come." And what happened the very year that Methuselah died? The flood came and covered the earth - God's judgment on sinful man.

3) Why would God wait 969 years to enact His judgment on man?

_____

_____

_____

_____

_____

God wants so very much for us to come to Him. He has given us gifts of "grace" and of "faith." He waited 969 years from when Methuselah was born. And when the ark was built, he waited another 7 days. God sent a redeemer to earth to die for our sins. He has waited a couple of thousand years since His Son died on the cross. How patient can he be?

God told Adam, in Genesis 2:17b. . . *in the day that you eat from it [the tree of the knowledge of good and evil] you will surely die.*

Genesis 5:5 *So all the days that Adam lived were nine hundred and thirty years, and he died.*

Because of Adam's original sin, we will all die a physical death. As we see through Genesis 5, all eventually died. God is true to His word. But, also, true to His word, God gave sinful man a redeemer. But, how patient will He be? Only God knows for sure....

Take it to Heart:

God gave Solomon anything he wished for.

If God gave you three wishes, what would you wish for?

Ingredients of Integrity

Genesis 6:1-9:17

Introduction

We live in a world of violence and corruption. In 1900, there was one murder for every 100,000 people in the United States of America. By 1974, that statistic had risen to one for every 10,000 people. That means that every year, one out of every 10,000 people in America die a victim of murder. In 1987, there were over 10,000,000 property crimes. In fact, the FBI (Federal Bureau of Investigation) stated that the likelihood of a person in America experiencing a violent crime has increased fifty percent in the last decade alone.

Violence has become a way of life. In fact, it is promoted in the standard media. By the time the average child reaches twelve years of age, he has watched 13,500 hours of television. That is twice as much time as he will spend in school. By the time he finishes that exposure, he has seen 14,000 deaths. That is one every hour. He has observed over 100,000 violent crimes. That is one every eight minutes. We are breeding a violence saturated generation.

Even the popular music of today and the rock culture is filled with lyrics suggesting violence. If you have believed the lie that every generation has its music, and this is the music for this generation, you need to see me, because I will let you see the lyrics. They have changed dramatically and evidently you are unaware. Perhaps that is why last year there were over 70,000 assaults against teachers in our public schools.

Violence is not the only problem in America. We have a problem with corruption, immorality, adultery, homosexuality, nudity, profanity and all are considered acceptable and are even portrayed by the media as legitimate lifestyles.

The unwed pregnancy rate among girls under the age of sixteen has increased eighty percent in the past ten years. In America, there are 10,000,000 alcoholics, and 1,000,000 of them are junior high kids. White collar crime has also risen dramatically in the last ten years. It is not surprising to hear of a banker, a financial investment group, an investor, or a religious leader being indicted for fraud, tax evasion, manipulation of interest, and downright embezzlement.

Now I have not listed these sins to get our sermon off to a great start or to be dramatic. I really want to answer a question that results from hearing just a few of the things that are happening in this country. The question is, "How in the world could I as an individual or us as a family survive the immorality of this generation? And not just survive, but how can we impact our generation for Jesus Christ?"

Four Essential Ingredients of Integrity

The solution is found in a story in the Bible. It is in Genesis 6, the story of Noah and his family. I want to discover with you today, ingredients of integrity that will help us not only survive the immorality and ungodliness of our generation, but help us to make a difference. We are not here to coast our way to heaven; we are here to make an impact as salt and light. How do we do that? We find the solution in Genesis 6:1-2.

Now it came about, when men began to multiply on the face of the land, and daughters were born to them, that the sons of God saw that the daughters of men were beautiful; and they took wives for themselves, whomever they chose.

Now there may be some who would like me to state a position on the debate that has been raised as to whether these were fallen angels or humans. Perhaps you have heard or been involved in such a discussion. I do not want to preach a sermon on this debate, but let me at least give a couple of reasons why I do not believe this is refers to the demonic world.

- First, if they were demons, they would not have been referred to as "the sons of God".

- Furthermore, if they were good angels that had not yet fallen, they would not be looking for or "on the prowl" for women. Satan and his horde had to leave heaven, and the angels remaining in heaven were being confirmed in their goodness by remaining with God.

- Thirdly, angels, according to Jesus in Matthew 22, do not have the ability to procreate – I believe that is the intention of that text. Procreation is a human phenomenon, a human miracle. God has given us the ability to procreate; to bear children.

Why? Because God promised that through this would come a Redeemer. Angels have no reason to procreate, they are beings created to worship God.

I think, the context in these verses would indicate that God has a problem not with fallen angels, but with men.

Notice verse 3.

Then the Lord said, "My spirit shall not strive with men forever, because he also is flesh; nevertheless his days shall be an hundred and twenty years."

I think this is a reference to the sons of God; the "ben Elohim"; the godly line of Seth. It is a godly line that is becoming weak. Why? Because they are intermarrying with ungodly women of the flesh – the ungodly line of Cain (that we are given in Genesis, chapter 4). So there is the intermingling of these two races that will bring about the necessity of judgment.

Well, enough of answering a question you probably you were not asking anyway. Let us continue with Genesis 6:5-9.

Then the Lord saw that the wickedness of man was great on the earth, and that every intent of the thoughts of his heart was only evil continually.

The Lord was sorry that He had made man on the earth, and He was grieved in His heart.

The Lord said, "I will blot out man whom I have created from the face of the land, from man to animals to creeping things and to birds of the sky; for I am sorry that I have made them."

(notice the word "But" in verse 8),

<u>But</u> Noah found favor in the eyes of the Lord.

These are the records of the generation of Noah. Noah was a righteous man, blameless in his time; Noah walked with God.

The word "blameless" could be translated, "a person of integrity". "Integrity" is defined as, "uprightness of character". Noah had it. However, that does not really tell us much about Noah, other than he was a man of great character.

Genesis 6:1-9:17

I want to give four ingredients of integrity that we can discover from this text. These ingredients are essential in your life and mine, if we are to ever survive the lure, the pull, the temptation, the obstacles to living a godly life in America today.

1. Integrity is purity in the midst of immorality

Look again at Genesis 6:5, and notice several characteristic words of this generation.

Then the Lord saw that the wickedness of man was great on the earth, and that __every__ intent of the __thoughts__ of his heart was __only__ __evil continually__.

What a sad lot. They never had a good thought in them. Every thought continually was only evil. This was the record of that generation.

Right in the middle of this corrupt, sinful world is a flickering light – Noah and his family, who were godly. His godliness was an indictment. In fact, I am convinced that a person of integrity will follow God even when it is unpopular. Noah discovered, in effect, when God was going to move, and he decided, when God came to him, that he would move with Him.

Hebrews 11 shows that Noah has entered into the "hall of faith". Look at Hebrews 11:7.

By faith Noah, being warned by God about things not yet seen, in reverence prepared an ark for the salvation of his household, by which he condemned the world, and became an heir of the righteousness which is according to faith.

There was Noah, an indictment upon his ungodly society. The words "he condemned the world," do not mean much to us, yet we use similar phrases all the time. We might say that, "we've got to fight the world" or "we're against the world".

What do they mean? These phrases are a reference to the world system. How is the world system engineered? The desires of perhaps fame, health, popularity, pleasure. All of these things grind the wheels of this world system into full gear. When we are an indictment on our world, what are we doing? We are living in such a way that we are not after these things or after these pleasures.

It says in this verse, that Noah rebuked or "condemned the world, and became an heir of the righteousness which is according to faith".

Why? Because Noah considered the approval of God more important than the applause of men.

How did Noah do that? Well, we know, through the chapters in Genesis, that he did it by his actions; that is, building an ark, and by what he said. The New Testament refers to Noah as "a preacher of righteousness" (II Peter 2:5). So, he not only lived a godly life, but he spoke the word.

There is a great debate today as to what generates the best kind of evangelism? Is it lifestyle evangelism or is it confrontational evangelism? Do you just live it and hope people get saved or do you pound people into the corner and ask them all the questions? Which do you appreciate most?

A man I respect was asked that question one time. He answered, "Well, let me ask you this question, 'Have you ever flown?'"

"Yeah, I have."

"Well, when you're 30,000 feet up, which do you appreciate most, the left wing or the right wing?"

"You appreciate both."

Noah did both, as evidenced in his life.

2. Integrity is obedience in the midst of ridicule.

Look at Genesis 6, again. Let us begin at verse 13 and read to the end of the chapter.

> *Then God said to Noah, "The end of all flesh has come before Me; for the earth is filled with violence because of them; and behold, I am about to destroy them with the earth.*
>
> *"Make for yourself an ark of gopher wood [or cedar wood]; you shall make the ark with rooms [could be translated nests], and shall cover it inside and outside with pitch."This is how you shall make it: the length of the ark three hundred cubits, its breadth fifty cubits, and its height thirty cubits.*

We do not know for certain what that measurement is, but we know that the ark will measure longer than one football field.

"You shall make a window for the ark, and finish it to a cubit from the top; and set the door of the ark in the side of it; you shall make it with lower, second, and third decks."

Now this boat looks a little bit different from the kind you and I have seen in our Sunday school material. This boat, when it was finished, looked more like a floating barge. It was almost square and was three stories high. It was like a box that floated. It has been discovered, when these measurements were tested, that it would have been virtually impossible for this vessel to capsize. That was important, because the tidal wave, the torrential rains, the hurricane-like weather was going to come, and this boat had to remain upright. Now continue to verse 17.

"Behold, I, even I am bringing the flood of water upon the earth, to destroy all flesh in which is the breath of life, from under heaven; everything that is on the earth shall perish.

"But I will establish My covenant with you; and you shall enter the ark – you and your sons and your wife, and your sons' wives with you.

(this is perhaps, an indication that the rest of the family will believe as well),

"And of every living thing of all flesh, you shall bring two of every kind into the ark, to keep them alive with you; they shall be male and female.

(by now, Noah is scratching his head),

"Of the birds after their kind, and of the animals after their kind, of every creeping thing of the ground after its kind [or species], two of every kind will come to you to keep them alive.

"As for you, take for yourself some of all food which is edible, and gather it to yourself; and it shall be for food for you and for them."

Then Noah said, "You must be joking. Are you serious, Lord?"

"I'm not joking."

Noah has just been asked to build a boat longer than a football field, and three stories high (approximately forty-five feet high). And, by the way, they were not building structures with stories until the

144

tower of Babel. It is also going to weigh about 18,000 tons and sit in his back yard somewhere. That is what God said to do.

(Chuckle) "Right!!"

Notice, as we continue to Genesis 6:22, that Noah's obedience was comprehensive.

Thus Noah did; according to <u>all</u> that God had commanded him, so he did.

Also notice Genesis 7:5.

Noah did according to <u>all</u> that the Lord had commanded him.

Look as well, at the last part of Genesis 7:9:

. . . as God had commanded Noah.

This was comprehensive obedience by Noah. In fact, the word "build" is the same Greek word used in the Septuagint and in the New Testament that is translated "prepared". Turn to Hebrews 9:1.

Now even the first covenant had regulations of divine worship and the earthly sanctuary.

Now, there is a tabernacle and as we continue in Hebrews, 9:2-5, the word "prepared" is used, which is the same word used of Noah. Notice the way the tabernacle is prepared.

For there was a tabernacle <u>prepared</u>, the outer one, in which were the lampstand and the table and the sacred bread; this is called the holy place.

Behind the second veil there was a tabernacle which is called the Holy of Holies,

having a golden altar of incense and the ark of the covenant covered on all sides with gold, in which was a golden jar holding the manna, and Aaron's rod which budded, and the tables of the covenant;

and above were the cherubim of glory overshadowing the mercy seat; but of these things we cannot now speak in detail.

In other words, there was such comprehensive detail that, when they came to make exactly what God specified, they did it with such care. That is the idea of Noah building an 18,000 ton boat.

You would think Noah would get some scraps and just put the thing together. He might staple and scotch tape and think, "We're going to make it – God will take care of us."

Absolutely not. Noah built that ark in such a way that the word used means he comprehensively obeyed every detail. And, nothing was lost.

Now, use your imagination for a moment. I can just hear a neighbor coming along, and I am sure Noah had them coming all the time, to see this thing Noah was building. This was the eighth wonder of the ancient world. This was on the tour maps of all the people in that area. I can just hear the neighbors, "What are you building, Noah?"

"I'm building an ark."

"What's an ark?"

"Well, I won't know until I finish it. I've never seen one before."

"Why are you building it, Noah?"

"It's going to rain."

"What's rain, Noah?"

"Well, I don't know. I haven't seen it yet."

"What does an ark do, Noah?"

"Well, I do know that, it floats on water."

"Floats on water? Noah, the nearest body of water, the Mediterranean Sea, is five hundred miles away. You missed it by a few miles. Wait. Did you say it floats like a boat? Let me see the specs to that thing."

I can just see the neighbor. Noah wrote it all down on the clay tablet because he did not want to miss a thing. This guy probably picks it up and says, "Ha! Who gave you these things?"

"God did."

"A lot God knows about building boats. He's left some things out."

"He did? Like what?"

"Well, there's no mention here of sails or oars. How you gonna move this thing?"

"Never thought about that."

"And also, you're missing probably the most important thing on a boat – you're missing a rudder. No mention of a rudder here. How you gonna steer it? Where's the pilot's wheel? Who's gonna navigate this thing?"

"I guess God will."

"Oh, and I suppose you've seen Him too."

"No, I've never seen God."

The reason I emphasize that particular point is because Hebrews 11:7, mentions that Noah believed "things not yet seen". He had never seen an ark. He had never seen rain. He had never seen God. But a man, or woman, of integrity is more interested in obeying the voice of God than, at times, the voice of reason.

Ladies, just imagine with me for a moment, how you would like to be married to a man who is considered the most eccentric, foolish man in the community? Think of it. I can just imagine Mrs. Noah going to the marketplace and all the ladies coming up, "Now, you dear poor soul, I'm sure you'll go with that basket case of a husband, you poor thing."

Kids, how would you like it if your dad was known as the biggest loser in the community? Don't answer that – you will be in trouble if you do! You would want to disown him, right? Unless, of course, you share his cause. And they did. Genesis 7:1 says,

> **Then the Lord said to Noah, "Enter the ark, you and all your household, for you alone I have seen to be righteous before Me in this time."**

Well, the ark is finished, and I know you are familiar with the story, so I will move along a little more quickly. They have finished perhaps, even bringing the animals, and have gone into the ark. I can imagine seeing Noah's family go into that ark.

If I had been Noah, about this time I would get my digs in. "I've been preaching for one hundred twenty years and nobody has responded. I've been called a fool and every other name in the book for one hundred twenty years. My kids have been ridiculed; made fun of, and my wife also."

Genesis 6:1-9:17

Now would be the chance. And yet, I would imagine Noah responding somewhat differently. I would imagine Noah, before entering the ark, turning around. I am sure crowds have gathered; crowds have come to see this thing. Noah's family has been hauling luggage and food from their home into the ark, and the crowds have come to watch. I would imagine that Noah would turn around. Now he is a suntanned man with deep lines in his face and calluses on his hands from hard labor. I would imagine one last time, he extends to them the invitation to enter the ark. He might say something like, "Don't you understand? Judgment is coming. Haven't you heard? Methuselah died. Won't you enter the ark?"

We know from the estimations of scientists and mathematicians that the ark was only half full. Half full – there was room for hundreds, if not thousands of people. Do you know how many people responded to his preaching, to his invitations, to his life – the kind of life you are living? Zero. It was a colossal failure. Noah only had seven converts – his own family members. That is one convert every seventeen years – boy, that is exciting. And yet, God considered him a man of integrity, not because people responded to his voice, but because he had responded to God's voice.

3.   Integrity is patience in the midst of uncertainty.

Look at Genesis 7:1-10.

Then the Lord said to Noah, "Enter the ark, you and all your household, for you alone I have seen to be righteous before Me in this time.

"You shall take with you of every clean animal by sevens, a male and his female; and of the animals that are not clean two, a male and his female;"

Understand that all of the animals are not going in two by two. The clean animals are going in by sevens; the unclean by twos. The reason for that is there would need to be animals for sacrifices. Continue to verse 3.

"also the birds of the sky, by sevens, male and female, to keep offspring alive on the face of all the earth.

(note the word "seven" in verse 4),

"For after <u>seven</u> more days, I will send rain on the earth forty days and forty nights; and I will blot out from the face of the land every living thing that I have made."

Noah did according to all that the Lord had commanded him.

Noah was six hundred years old when the flood of water came upon the earth.

Then Noah and his sons and his wife and his sons' wives with him entered the ark because of the water of the flood.

Of clean animals and animals that are not clean and birds and everything that creeps on the ground,

there went into the ark to Noah by twos, male and female, as God had commanded Noah.

(see verse 10),

It came about after the seven days, that the water of the flood came upon the earth.

That is why I call this patience in the midst of uncertainty. I cannot believe the obedience of Noah; the patience of Noah and his family. They have gotten everyone into the ark, they are in there surrounded by animals, and guess what happens? For seven days, absolutely nothing! The door is shut; they have all their equipment; they are ready to float – but there is no rain.

I imagine after a day or two, the neighbors lose their uncertainty; they get a little more bold. They had been wondering, "Is judgment coming?" Now two days have passed and nothing is happening. Now they are out at the ark barbecuing. One man said they are playing badminton using the ark as the net. They are out there having a great time and hollering, "Hey, Noah, are you still in there?"

Noah is probably scratching his head, thinking, "Lord, is this some kind of sham? Where's the rain?"

Yet, there is no record of that. Although Noah was probably confused and uncertain, there is no record that he ever questioned God.

My friends, integrity believes God even when it seems ridiculous. You and I want integrity as long as it makes us look respectable. Noah was willing to follow integrity, even when it made him look ridiculous.

Look at verse 10 again.

It came about after the seven days, that the water of the flood came upon the earth.

I think this was probably God's way of saying, "Look, I'm going to give mankind seven more days to repent. Seven more days because, when all of the generations read of My judgment, they're going to know that I was so patient with man. I gave him every opportunity, and he would not repent."

Now look at Genesis 7:17 through the end of the chapter.

Then the flood came upon the earth for forty days, and the water increased and lifted up the ark, so that it rose above the earth.

The water prevailed and increased greatly upon the earth, and the ark floated on the surface of the water.

The water prevailed more and more upon the earth, so that all the high mountains everywhere under the heavens were covered.

(This is a universal flood, not a local flood.),

The water prevailed fifteen cubits higher, and the mountains were covered.

All flesh that moved on the earth perished, birds and cattle and beasts and every swarming thing that swarms upon the earth, and all mankind;

of all that was on the dry land, all in whose nostrils was the breath of the spirit of life, died.

Thus He blotted out every living thing that was upon the face of the land, from man to animals to creeping things and to birds of the sky, and they were blotted out from the earth; and only Noah was left, together with those that were with him in the ark.

The water prevailed upon the earth one hundred and fifty days.

You need to understand that Noah and his family will float in this thing for over a year. This is not a weekend trip; this is a year plus. And when the ark finally grounds on top of one of the ridges in the mountain ranges of Ararat, God did not tell Noah, "All right, here are all the details of how you begin."

God never told Noah what life would be like after the flood. He never even told Noah how long he would float. Noah is sending out a dove to look for some kind of dry land. Noah is so patient that he sends out a dove and waits seven days. I would have been sending out doves every thirty minutes to look for some kind of dry land. What a patient man. In the midst of uncertainty, Noah was a man of integrity.

4. Integrity is worship in the midst of difficulty.

Read chapter 8:14-19.

In the second month, on the twenty-seventh day of the month, the earth was dry.

Then God spoke to Noah, saying,

"Go out of the ark, you and your wife and your sons and your sons' wives with you.

"Bring out with you every living thing of all flesh that is with you, birds and animals and every creeping thing that creeps on the earth, that they may breed abundantly on the earth, and be fruitful and multiply on the earth."

So Noah went out, and his sons and his wife and his sons' wives with him.

Every beast, every creeping thing, and every bird, everything that moves on the earth, went out by their families from the ark.

And Noah kind of threw his arms out and said, "Finally, this is over. Lord, *never* put me through that again."

No, we are told in verse 20,

Then Noah built an altar to the Lord, and took of every clean animal and of every clean bird and offered burnt offerings on the altar.

The first thing Noah did was lead his family in worship. What a confusing year this had been for him. It was a year of silence from God; a year of uncertainty; a year of tremendous difficulty, and yet, he worships God.

151

What About Today?

God responds in Genesis 9, by establishing the Noahic covenant, a covenant that will change some of the things on planet earth.

One of the covenant changes will be that animals will now live in fear of mankind. Man and beast will now be carnivorous.

The beautiful thing about the Noahic covenant, as we know, is the establishment of the rainbow as the sign of the covenant. By that, God says, "Every time you look up into the heavens, the earth will never be covered again by water." And by the way, you and I see the evidence of the covenant as well.

The unbeliever says, "Well, that's great – Noah is a wonderful man and he lived in a wicked world, but there is no need for a Noah today. God's judgment is not coming today."

Turn with me to II Peter 3:3-7. Sinful man refuses talk of judgment, but note what the scriptures clearly state.

Know this first of all, that in the last days . . .

(that is our generation, our day, our age of grace),

. . . mockers will come with their mocking, following after their own lusts,

and saying, "Where is the promise of His coming? For ever since the fathers fell asleep, all continues just as it was from the beginning of creation."

For when they maintain this, it escapes their notice that by the word of God the heavens existed long ago and the earth was formed out of water and by water,

through which the world at that time was destroyed, being flooded with water.

But by His word the present heavens and earth are being reserved for . . .

(for what kind of judgment?),

. . . fire, kept for the day of judgment and destruction of ungodly men.

Skip to verse 12.

looking for and hastening the coming of the day of God, because of which the heavens will be destroyed by burning, and the elements will melt with intense heat!

Just as certainly as God kept His word and the flood came, and He gave mankind centuries to believe through the preaching of Enoch and Noah, so He has given us a day of grace to believe, but judgment is also coming. How is it coming this time? Fire.

Someone might say, "Ha, ha, ha! How's that going to happen?"

Who knows? They asked the same thing about the water in Noah's day, and yet it came. My friends, do you understand that one of the most popular, fastest growing theological errors in our day is the disbelief and rejection of judgment; a literal hell? Yet, God says it will come.

Two parallels between Noah's ark and Jesus Christ

Let me give two obvious parallels between Noah's ark and Jesus Christ, which is a sermon in itself. This is a wonderful illustration and picture of salvation.

1. The first parallel is that God, not man, designed the ark simply, yet profoundly, as His plan of salvation to all who would enter.

What is the ark of salvation today? For all who are in who? Christ Jesus. As Romans 8:1 tells us,

. . . there is now no condemnation for those who are in Christ Jesus.

2. The second obvious parallel is that the ark only had one door.

Jesus would say in John 10: 9,

I am the door; if anyone enters through Me, he will be saved .

If you are a believer today, it is possible in this corrupt generation, to be a person of integrity. However, it will take a pursuit of Jesus Christ as Lord. That pursuit will develop in you:

- purity in the midst of immorality;
- obedience in the midst of ridicule;
- patience in the midst of uncertainty;
- worship in the midst of difficulty.

Oh, how we need men, women, and young people of integrity today.

Dudley Tyng was a well known speaker in the 1800's. In 1858, he spoke to five thousand young men at the Young Men's Christian Association. We know it today as the YMCA, but it is no longer Christian. Dudley preached to five thousand, and one thousand people responded to Christ. He was a young man.

Later that day, he went back to the farm and decided to go to the barn and watch the men shelling corn. As he was watching, he got a little too close to the machine. His jacket got caught and his arm was pulled into the grinding gears of the machine. It was lacerated beyond repair. In a few hours, he would die. Medicine, at that time, was too primitive and the loss of blood was too great.

As he lay in bed, the people surrounding him suggested that Dudley give a word to those who listened to his message; to those who were following Christ; to those thousands of people that he was influencing. They said, "Dudley, give us a message to take back to the people."

They say that he strained and then said, "Tell the people to stand up for Jesus."

That night, the hall was filled as they relayed the story of Dr. Tyng and his death, and gave the message that he had given them.

The poem was written that we sing, with the words,

Stand up, stand up for Jesus, ye soldiers of the cross;

Lift high His royal banner, it must not suffer loss.

From victory unto victory His army shall He lead,

Till every foe is vanquished and Christ is Lord indeed.

That is what it takes to truly pursue integrity. That is the battle of integrity.

Ingredients of Integrity

Ingredients of Integrity

Genesis 6:1-9:17

Digging Deeper :

Genesis 6:8 *__But__ Noah found favor in the eyes of the Lord. These are the records of the generation of Noah. Noah was a righteous man, blameless in his time; Noah walked with God.*

Noah is **blameless**. Noah **walked with God**....Notice how the two phrases compliment and support each other. Can a man be blameless and **NOT** be walking with God? Can a man have integrity and not be walking with God? When Adam fell, man fell into a life of sin. Man's natural motivation is for man's *wants* and for man's *glory*. The lure of the man-centered or self-centered life is too great for us to overcome. We must depend on God for the strength. We must walk with God if we are to be blameless and if we are to have integrity.

1) List 5 qualities that you believe define **Integrity** in a person. Relate these qualities to a person **walking with God.**

_____

_____

_____

_____

_____

_____

_____

_____

How can we be expected to have integrity given the immoral world in which we live? We have grown up in a culture that tells us that everything is "OK" as long as it pleases us. We are told that we should look within ourselves for the answers to right and wrong - within us is the "power." Genesis tells us that within us is the tainted "seed" of Adam. Is that the "power" that we want to bring up? If we look within ourselves for the answers to right and wrong, we'll find the answers that Satan has planted there.

Genesis 6:5 *Then the Lord saw that the wickedness of man was great on the earth, and that <u>every</u> intent of the <u>thoughts</u> of his heart was <u>only</u> <u>evil continually</u>*

So, we must take a stand. Noah took a stand. He *"condemned the world."* He took a stand against the world and the "norms" of that society.

2) List 5 things that "society" has thrown at you this week and describe both how normal society would react to these and also how a person that "walks with God," should react to these.

_____

_____

_____

_____

_____

_____

_____

_____

_____

_____

Throughout history people have been persecuted for their beliefs. Many have been killed. Many have been imprisoned and tortured. Many have been willing to endure these trials for their faith. On a smaller scale, neighbors or acquaintances might not understand the Christian faith. They see a Christian and want to question why he or she would follow a God by faith. Why would a Christian go against the "norm" of society. When the rest of the world is listening to music with lyrics that glorify Satan, not God, when the rest of the world condones pornography and lifestyles opposite from God's word, what does the man or woman of **"true"** faith do? The Christian is commanded to follow God. The Christian must stand firm against the lure of a fallen society. This is **Integrity.** When we commit ourselves to follow Jesus Christ by faith and we lean on God to keep us from the evils of the world, then it can be said that we have **Integrity.** We have made a commitment, a promise, and we stick to that commitment in good times and tough times. Even when people all around us may scoff at us and may laugh at us and may ridicule us, we stand firm for Jesus Christ through faith in Him.

Look at Noah, a man of integrity. He was building an ark for a coming flood that no one could see coming. He was, by faith, listening to God for guidance. Sure the scoffers were there. Sure the world told him he was crazy. Noah had made a commitment to follow God and he stuck to his commitment – **A man with Integrity.**

Genesis 7:5 *Noah did according to all that the Lord had commanded him.*

Noah built the ark and did as God commanded. He brought the animals into the ark and then he waited. **Patience** is certainly a test of faith. Noah waited seven days for the rains to begin. What do you think his thoughts were during this time? What would your thoughts be? Finally the floods came. God did exactly what He said he was going to do. **Patience** to stay the course and stick to your commitments when everything around you is pulling you a different way, that's **Integrity.**

Genesis 7:10 *It came about after the seven days, that the water of the flood came upon the earth.*

What did Noah do after the flood subsided and they left the ark? He worshipped God.

3) Even through everything, Noah first thought to worship God. Why is this important for a person of Integrity?

_____

_____

_____

Take it to Heart :

We as Christians can use the faith of Noah as he built the ark as an example for our faith. He did not see rain coming. He continued to work while those around him must have mocked and ridiculed him. And even when he finished building the ark, his faith had to remain strong until the rain finally came. And what an ordeal he went through for a year. But, when it was over, he worshipped God. Noah was a true man of integrity.

How is your integrity today?

Are you able to stand up to the ridicule of non believers?

How patient are you?

God has given us the gift of **faith.** We can take His gift and use it to trust in Him. Even while all around us is decaying, we can stand tall for God. We too can have **integrity...**but only with help from **Jesus.**

159

Lessons From Sinning Saints

Genesis 9:20-11:25

Introduction

After our discussion today, the rest of the book of Genesis will only cover three hundred fifty years, yet it is the majority of the book. It deals primarily with Abraham and Joseph.

Today, we come, in Genesis 9, to an unfortunate passage of scripture. While in our last study we discussed the ingredients of integrity, today we will have a lesson from a sinning saint. Unfortunately, both lessons revolve around the same individual. That reminds us that anyone can sin. In fact, no one is above sin or temptation – not even someone like Noah.

Exposition

Look at Genesis 9:20-29. This is after the flood, when Noah's family had disembarked from the ark.

Then Noah began farming and planted a vineyard.

He drank of the wine and became drunk, and uncovered himself inside his tent.

Ham, the father of Canaan, saw the nakedness of his father, and told his two brothers outside.

But Shem and Japheth took a garment and laid it upon both their shoulders and walked backward and covered the nakedness of their father; and their faces were turned away, so that they did not see their father's nakedness.

When Noah awoke from his wine, he knew what his youngest son had done to him.

(so he prophetically declared),

So he said, "Cursed be Canaan; a servant of servants He shall be to his brothers."

He also said, "Blessed be the Lord, the God of Shem, and let Canaan be his servant.

"May God enlarge Japheth, and let him dwell in the tents of Shem; and let Canaan be his servant."

Noah lived three hundred and fifty years after the flood.

So all the days of Noah were nine hundred and fifty years, and he died.

Sin . . . in the life of Noah

The parallel between Noah and Adam is interesting. The first man to ever live, Adam, sinned by partaking of the literal fruit of the vine. Noah, the first man after the flood, would also sin by drinking the fruit of the vine. Both men would fall and, as a result, one would recognize his nakedness, the other would become naked. Both would receive a covering from someone else, and, as a result of that sin, both would receive a curse. And yet, in that curse, would also be the promise of blessing.

Now the sins of Noah were two-fold:

- First, Noah became drunk, and drunkenness was in violation of God's command, especially as you read later in the Old Testament.

- Secondly, not only did he become drunk, Noah became naked; that is, he, in his lewdness that we dare not even imagine, perhaps in his tent, shed his clothing in drunkenness.

Noah, this man of God, the preacher of righteousness, was now drunk and naked. He was shamefully exposing himself.

I found, in fact, at least six different interpretations of this passage of scripture. The interpretation that I will follow is that which literally follows the meaning of the Hebrew words. I know there is safety in discovering what the literal text means.

The words in verse 21, "uncovered himself," are the same Hebrew words used in scripture for "shameful exposure". There is nothing particularly sensational in this – Noah became drunk and took off his clothing; perhaps lewdly dancing about.

The confusion is in what Ham did. Some would suggest at least six different interpretations of this. Perhaps he had an incestuous relationship with Noah; that is, he uncovered his nakedness being a Hebrew idiom of lying with his wife. The text, however, does not indicate that. Some have even suggested that there is a homosexual violation. Yet the text does not say that Ham uncovered the nakedness of Noah, but that Noah uncovered his own nakedness.

So, what did Ham do? Verse 24 says,

> **When Noah awoke from his wine, he knew what his youngest son [Ham] had done to him.**

Let me give two things that Ham did. Notice verse 22 again.

> **Ham, the father of Canaan, saw the nakedness of his father, and told his two brothers outside.**

- First, Ham saw.

The Hebrew meaning of the word is that he gazed; he observed; he watched. He is perhaps behind some covering of the tent, and he is watching his father.

  - Not only that, I think the real sin was in what follows. The Hebrew word "told" means literally, "with delight". Ham was really enjoying this.

This was not only dishonoring the honor of his father, but perhaps, was even revealing that in his heart, he had repudiated the faith of his father. "Ha! This is the preacher of righteousness. Look at what he's doing." and he was delighted in his father's fall.

The only thing that is worse than committing a specific sin perhaps, is the devilish delight in observing that sin in someone else and sharing it with others. Why do you think the tabloids make millions of dollars every year? Because they pander to the fallen nature of man that delights in the sorry side, the seedy side of humanity. So their stories are of the fights, the break ups, the divorces, the lawsuits, and all of the seedy things that happen, the tragic things that happen to mankind.

So, Noah awakens from his stupor and makes a prophetic curse. Look at verse 24 again.

> *When Noah awoke from his wine, he knew what his youngest son had done to him.*

Noah knew Ham had mocked him and he makes a prophetic curse; that is, he is saying what will happen. He is not saying, "Okay, Canaan, or Ham, you are now going to do this," he is saying, "I perceive by revelation that this will be your future."

So, Noah gives the curse and in it, is also the promise. Look at verse 26a again.

He also said, "Blessed be the Lord, the God of Shem . . .

Shem would be the father of the Semites. You can see in the name "Shem" the word "Sem". This is Semite nations from which Israel would come. So, this is the promise of the coming Messiah.

Japheth is the father of the Indo-European nations, from which the majority of Americans have come. Ham will become the father of the African, the Egyptian, and the Arabian nations. This is easily found in documented accounts – not only in biblical records, but in accounts by secular anthropologists.

By the way, nations, or the idea of nationality, are God's idea. Turn in your Bible to the book of Acts. It has been interesting and has given me great comfort to discover this in Acts 17. Look at verses 24 through 27a. Paul is speaking in the Areopagus to the philosophers. He is referring to the "unknown god".

The God who made the world and all things in it, since He is Lord of heaven and earth, does not dwell in temples made with hands;

nor is he served by human hands, as though he needed anything, since He Himself gives to all people life and breath and all things;

(note verses 26 and 27a),

and He made from one man every nation of mankind to live on all the face of the earth, having determined their appointed times . . .

(that is, how long they will last as a nation),

. . . and the boundaries of their habitation,

(that is, how large they will grow; how much land or territory they will conquer before crumbling),

that they would seek God, if perhaps they might grope for Him and find Him . . .

What is the purpose of the nations today? They are visual lessons that you and I, as part of a nation, need to search for God; to follow God.

What did great Rome teach us? What did Babylon teach us? They teach us that when we reject God, He rejects us.

What will the historians write of America one day? That, we, as a nation, began to reject God. And, that He would then reject us. He will allow us to bear the consequences of our own immorality, and like Rome, crumble from within.

Slavery . . . in the future of Canaan

Now look again at Genesis 9. There are some people who believe the Africans or the black peoples are consigned to slavery and that God even ordained it as such in this curse. I have even heard that from evangelical lips.

There is one very clear way of discovering whether that is true or not – read what the text says. I do not mean to be facetious or caustic, yet it is tragic that this view, among others, is the result of a simple misunderstanding, if not ignorance of what the text says.

Carefully read verse 25 again.

. . . Cursed be Canaan; a servant of servants he shall be to his brothers.

Who is cursed – Ham and all of his descendants? No. Canaan is cursed – one branch of the descendants of Ham, not all of the descendants of Ham. Only one branch is cursed, and that is Canaan. Canaan would be the forefather of all the Canaanites.

Do you remember the Canaanites? They inhabited the land which God had promised to Israel. When Joshua led the people into Canaan, what did they have to do? Subjugate; overthrow; bring under their authority who? The Canaanites.

From the Canaanites came the Hittites, Perizzites, the Amorites, the Jebusites, and all the other "ites". All of these came from Canaan, and now in fact, they have ceased to exist as a nation. The curse has been fulfilled.

If anyone had a claim to this curse in this century, by the way, it would not be the African; it would be the Arab who lives in Palestine.

Now, I have mentioned the descendants of Ham and Shem, so what about Japheth? Let me give some interesting facts about his descendants.

In Genesis 9:27, we are told that God would "enlarge Japheth". Enlarging means that he would conquer, he would enlarge his borders. That is exactly what happened. Let me share a few thoughts with you.

Japheth's son Gomer, who is mentioned in Genesis 10:2-3, is the forefather of the Germans – that is where we get that nation. One of Gomer's sons, Togarmah, established Turkey. They always named their nations after themselves, being modest as they were. In fact, the Armenians came to be called the House of Targam.

Especially interesting are three of Japheth's sons mentioned in Genesis 10:2.

The sons of Japheth were Gomer and Magog and Madai and Javan and Tubal and Meshech and Tiras.

Now Magog, Tubal, and Meshech have given us the northern people, or the Russians. In fact, Ezekiel mentions Magog, in chapter 38, as the prince of Rosh. The Hebrew word for "chief prince" is the word "rosh," or "rush," from which we get our English word "Russia".

Now, by the way, we are not talking about millions of years ago, we are talking about four thousand years ago. This is clearly seen in the histories kept by man, and especially in this table of nations.

Now the two tribes of Tubal and Meshech are found in the writings of Herodotus. He indicated that by his time, the names had developed into Mesken and Theobelian. These two tribes would push north and east of the Black Sea into what is now Russia. In fact, these two tribes are now used as the dividing marks of the modern state of Russia. Tubal is now Tobol on the Tobolsk River and Mesken is now Moscow on the Moskva River.

It is fascinating to me, that this was the beginning of that which would one day rise up against Israel. These are the writings of Paul. That God made every nation and He appointed not only their times; that is, how long they will exist, but also their boundaries. God is in total control. He is not only the creator of nations; He is the controller of nations. I do not mean to imply by that that America is safe from the Russians. I do not find America in our text, but what I do find is the sovereign God who has mapped out even the nations and their boundaries.

Separation . . . in the course of history

Now turn to Genesis 11, which introduces the story of the tower of Babel. This is a story of great mystery. It is fairly well documented that astrology and even the zodiac and idolatry ultimately trace their roots back to Nimrod and his kingdom of Babylon.

Note where Babylon got its start. Turn back to Genesis 10:8-10a.

Now Cush became the father of Nimrod; he became a mighty one on the earth. He was a mighty hunter before the Lord; . .

("in the face of the Lord," it should say),

. . . therefore it is said, "Like Nimrod a mighty hunter before the Lord." The beginning of his kingdom was Babel . . .

This is a spite; this is hunting in spite of the face of the Lord. Nimrod is the first man to be called "mighty," and these verses refer to his prowess in hunting – not animals, but the souls of men that he will use in building his kingdom of Babylon. In fact, his name "Nimrod" means, "let us rebel".

Nimrod's father Cush, had heard the curse and said, "I am not going to abide by that. My little boy will grow up one day to be the rebuilder; the rebuilder of a nation." and thus, we have Nimrod.

Turn to Genesis 11:1-3.

Now the whole earth used the same language and the same words. It came about as they journeyed east, that they found a plain in the land of Shinar and settled there. They said to one another, "Come, let us make bricks and burn them thoroughly." And they used brick for stone, and they used tar for mortar.

The next verse is a violation of God's command that we read in Genesis 9, to replenish or fill the entire earth. Look at verse 4a.

They said, "Come, let us build for ourselves a city and a tower whose top will reach into heaven . . ."

This "into heaven" could be translated "atop". This is their religious system; this is replacing God. This tower will reach the heavens – that was their declaration. Continue to verse 4b and notice what they said.

". . . and let us make for ourselves a name, otherwise we will be scattered abroad over the face of the whole earth."

This tower was a monument erected to symbolize their rebellion against the command of God. Archeologists have discovered these towers, like the ziggurats, and they have found that at the top of these towers were altars and rooms dedicated to the worship of the signs of the zodiak. In fact, they have found these symbols painted and drawn on the walls. So, what we have today in modern astrology is not modern, it is going back in its roots to the ultimate rebellion that God would one day, in this chapter, come to stop.

Let me read something rather interesting from a man who has studied this. He says the text speaks of the top of the tower as being that which was dedicated to the heavens as a place of worship. So, astrology, which focuses on the study of the zodiac, originated in Babylon. If you look at any book on astrology, you will find that it was the Chaldeans, which is another name for the inhabitants of Babylon, who first developed the zodiac by dividing the sky into sections and giving meanings to each on the basis of the stars that are found there. A person's destiny is said to be determined by whatever section or sign he is under.

Do you know what your sign is, by the way? I think most of us have stumbled into that knowledge which points its finger back to rebellion against God.

Let me continue. From Babylon, astrology passed to the empire of ancient Egypt, where it mingled with animism and polytheism. The pyramids were constructed with certain mathematical relationships to the stars. The sphinx – that huge monument that is still in Egypt today, and if you have ever toured there, you have seen it – has astrological significance. It has the head of a woman, symbolizing Virgo, the virgin, and the body of a lion, symbolizing Leo. Virgo is the first sign of the zodiac; Leo is the last. So the sphinx, which actually means "joining" in Greek, is the meeting point of the zodiac. The sphinx is symbolizing, in effect, that this is the beginning and the end. It is saying, "Our religious system is eternal. It is the alpha, the beginning, and the omega, the ending."

False religion, even way back in the time of Nimrod, sought to obliterate the true beginning and end. It is interesting that when Jesus Christ comes to rule, He will state, as we are told in the latter part of Revelation, chapters 21 and 22, "I am the Alpha and the Omega, the beginning and the end."

I would issue this warning, if you read the horoscopes – stop, it is a dangerous thing. It traces its roots back to the idolatry of Babylon.

Well, God confounds the language. Look at Genesis 11:5-9.

The Lord came down to see the city and the tower which the sons of men had built. The Lord said, "Behold, they are one people, and they all have the same language. And this is what they began to do, and now nothing which they purpose to do . . .

(that is, evil),

". . . will be impossible for them. Come, let Us . . .

(perhaps an indication of the Trinity),

". . . go down and there confuse their language, so that they will not understand one another's speech." So the Lord scattered them abroad from there over the face of the whole earth; and they stopped building the city.

That was the plan of God, "I don't want you erecting a one world government. I don't want you to have one city ruling all the world. I want you to scatter and develop into the nations that I have designed."

So, He came down and took care of that which even today, would create a common barrier; that is, language. It is hard enough to understand each other even when we speak English, much less when there is are other languages.

I read an illustration of this point by a pastor. A lady in his congregation was a kindergarten teacher. It snowed a lot where she taught, and snowsuits were required. One day she was, with a lot of difficulty, helping a little boy into his snowsuit. It was one of those with all the ties, snaps, and buttons. It took her about five minutes. Finally, when she got the boy in it, he looked up at her and said, "This isn't my snowsuit."

So, with the grace of kindergarten teachers, who deserve a medal of honor anyway, she pulls the snowsuit off this boy, after untying and unsnapping everything. She finally gets him out . . . and he continues his story, "This is my sister's snowsuit, but my mother said I could wear it today."

If I had been that teacher, there would be one less kid on planet earth!

There is great difficulty in communicating. In fact, the coming kingdom is prophesied in Zephaniah 3:9 (KJV), where God says through him,

For then [in the kingdom] will I turn to the people a pure language, that they may all call upon the name of the Lord, to serve Him with one consent.

Isn't it fascinating to know that in heaven, we will all once again have the same language. The Spanish, the Chinese, the Mexicans, the Americans will all be able to communicate with one language, and I think, communicate perfectly.

Application

Now I want to take a practical turn in this sermon. Let me give several things that will be helpful from this passage, unfortunate as it is.

One thing was perfectly clear to me, as I studied this passage – had we written the Bible, we would have left out the sins of the patriarchs. There would have been things that we would have ignored, but God does not. In fact, I think that is another proof that God determined the content of this Book.

Sometimes the Bible is so comprehensive that it is embarrassing. Sometimes it probes, and we wonder why. We wonder why the Lord gave us these last five verses of Noah's life. Why not end on a good note? Because I think God wants us to learn not only from the successes of the saints, but from their failures as well.

Seven lessons from the sins of Noah

1. The first lesson is that a believer is never immune to sin

Noah was six hundred years old when the flood came, and he had lived his life righteously for six hundred years. Then, in his later years, he mars his perfect record.

Is this unique in the Bible? Absolutely not. Moses, in his later years, struck the rock declaring for himself glory due only to God. When David was in his fifties, he fell into immorality.

2. Past success does not guarantee future safety from sin.

You do not inoculate yourself by all of the successes of the past week. Satan does not say, "Well, you know, he's been really good this past week. We won't bother him this week."

Nor does Satan say, "Well, that person is almost in heaven. Let's leave him alone."

No, the temptation to sin persists to the grave.

3. Small temptations are often the most dangerous.

Look at Noah – the preacher of righteousness. He was a man who for a hundred and twenty years, said "No" to all kinds of immorality. Then, with a cheap flask of homemade wine, he is brought to his knees.

It was a small temptation, and yet, it was the most dangerous. Perhaps that is what the writer of scripture means, in I Corinthians 10:12, when he says,

> *. . . let him who thinks he stands take heed that he does not fall.*

Watch out for the little things.

4. Temptations are always changing faces.

By the time you master one temptation, another one comes along. I say "changing faces" because ultimately, all temptation asks the same question, "Whose voice are you going to listen to – the voice of God or the voice of the world system, your flesh, and Satan?"

5. Sin never affects the sinner alone.

This is probably one of the most tragic parts of sin. It never affects just the sinner. You might say, "Oh no, my sin isn't affecting anyone but me. In fact, no one even knows."

However, it is that sin in your life that keeps you from being the kind of husband, father, believer, testimony that you should be. Someone is robbed when you and I get away from what God would have us to be.

Someone wrote, "Sin is like a pebble thrown into a pond of water. Although the pebble strikes only one place, the ripples from its force stretch outward."

Genesis 9:20-11:25

6. Believers never have an excuse for sin.

I stress "believers" because I Corinthians 10:13 says,

No temptation has overtaken you but such as is common to man; and God is faithful, who will not allow you to be tempted beyond what you are able, but with the temptation will provide the way of escape also, so that you will be able to endure it.

When we sin, we say "No" to God's escape plan.

7. God never ignores sin.

God never ignores sin, even in the life of a saint. God never plays favorites. Sin will always bring guilt, no matter who you may be. That guilt may bring the loss of joy; the loss of fellowship – there are always consequences.

Two lessons from our own sin nature

There are two further lessons that we can learn from our own biography of sin that God has given us. We are like Noah. Although we are not in the scriptures, we can certainly see the similarities that reside in our sin nature. Let me give two very positive lessons that we can learn from our sin nature.

I know that sounds odd that there is something positive to be learned about our sin nature. There is, but notice, I did not say "sin". There is nothing positive about sin. I do not want anyone to call me this week and say, "Pastor, I sinned. And man, you're right, I learned that positive lesson."

I said "sin nature". God can use the awareness of our nature to sin to do two things.

1. Lesson number one is that the awareness of our sin nature can be used by God to develop appreciation for our position in Christ.

Paul, the great apostle, cried to God in Romans 7:19-24 (paraphrased),

Lord, whatever I want to do, I can't do it. Whatever I don't want to do, it seems like that's what I'm always doing. Who will deliver me from this body of death? Who will excise from me the sinful nature?

172

The body of death is referring to a Roman custom. A man who had committed murder was taken to the cross. Before he was put on that cross, if the murdered victim was a slave or someone of ill repute or perhaps, not a Roman citizen, the dead body would be laid on top of the murderer and strapped to him neck to neck, wrist to wrist, waist to waist, leg to leg, and then, put on the cross. That is what is referred to as this body of death. The murderer would die a hideous death with his victim cheek to cheek.

So, Paul says, in verse 24b,

. . . Who will set me free from the body of this death?

In other words, "Who will set me free from this wicked old man; this old nature that is strapped to me?"

Paul's awareness of his sin was so great, but then he concludes with Romans 7:25a, and Romans 8:1,

Thanks be to God through Jesus Christ our Lord! . . . there is now no condemnation for those who are in Christ Jesus.

2. Lesson number two is that the awareness of our sin nature can be used by God not only to develop our appreciation for our position in Christ, but to develop our gratitude for Christ's work in us.

II Corinthians 5:17 tells us,

Therefore if anyone is in Christ, he is a new creature; the old things [continually] passed away; behold, new things have [continually] come.

We get the idea that when someone – scruffy, unshaven, dirty – becomes a believer and the next week, he is in church – three piece suit, Bible in hand – then, yes, he is a believer. No, no – it is a Christian life, and it takes a life. It is not the Christian moment. One of the things about our sin nature is that it develops in us the appreciation that Jesus Christ is at work in our lives. There is so much that needs to be changed. There is so much developing that can take place. Do not expect changes in everything in a moment – it takes a life.

However, be confident that, as we are told in Philippians 2:13,

. . . it is God who is at work in you, both to will and to work for His good pleasure.

I like what Paul says in Philippians 1:6,

. . . I am confident of this very thing, that He who began a good work in you will perfect it until the day of Jesus Christ.

God is at work. Our sin nature is a lesson. The reason that you and I are miserable in our sin is simply because Jesus Christ gives us the sense of guilt. It is our relationship with Him that shows us our wickedness. Thank God for that. It is a dangerous situation when an individual has no sense of sin.

Do you fail? Yes. Do you sin? Yes. But you know your sins are forgiven, because you gave your life to Jesus Christ. Isaiah 1:18a tells us,

. . . Though your sins are as scarlet, they will be as white as snow . . .

This is the story of Noah – a saint and a sinner. Did he fail? Yes. Did he sin? Yes. God gave the story to us so that we might learn. Yet God would write Noah's epithet in Hebrews 11:7,

By faith Noah . . . became an heir of the righteousness which is according to faith.

We too have the righteousness of God, if we have come to the cross of Jesus Christ.

Lessons From Sinning Saints

Lessons From Sinning Saints

Genesis 9:20-11:25

Digging Deeper:

> Romans 3:23 *for all have sinned and fall short of the glory of God,*

Noah was chosen by God to build the ark. He was the man that stood against the world and his faith in God was very strong. But, every man will sin. Noah came from Adam's seed and just as Adam had done at the beginning of the earth, Noah repeated after the flood. Noah sinned.

> Genesis 9:21 *He drank of the wine and became drunk, and uncovered himself inside his tent.*

As incredible as Noah's faith was, he still could not resist the temptation of sin. If a man like Noah gives in to Satan, then how do we have a chance? We can not resist temptation on our own. We must depend on the Holy Spirit that dwells in us as believers. The Holy Spirit will guide us and help us want to stay focused on God. But, we must give ourselves totally to God for the Holy Spirit to work effectively in us. We have all of the Holy Spirit that we will ever need, but the real question is, "How much does the Holy Spirit have of us?"

1) What were Ham's sins? And what were his curses?

_____

_____

_____

_____

176

Man searches for a god. If man rebels against the one **true** God, he will search for something to take God's place. Man will create many gods to fulfill this desire to worship something.

Genesis 9:4 *They said, "Come, let us build for ourselves a city and a tower whose top will reach into heaven and let us make for ourselves a name, otherwise we will be scattered abroad over the face of the whole earth."*

Cush and his son Nimrod were separated from God. Thus, they searched for their own god. They decided to build a city of their own. And they decided to try to rebuild their cursed nation. All of this was against God's will. The tower they were building was to reach up into heaven or literally they intended to create something that would reach into and on top of heaven. They were trying to build their own religion and by building the tower into heaven, they wanted to prove that this new religion was equal to God. God had cursed them and forever made them separate from Him. Thus, they are searching for someone or something to take His place.

This same problem has been demonstrated throughout the years. False religions proliferate through out the world. All of these false religions have one thing in common. They worship a false god. They do not worship the one **true** God. They have separated from God

2) Name 3 false religions that are in existence today. And name the false god that they worship.

_____

_____

_____

_____

Zephaniah 3:9 (KJV) *For then [in the kingdom] will I turn to the people a pure language, that they may all call upon the name of the Lord, to serve Him with one consent.*

That is good news that we find in Zephaniah. One day God will bring all the believers together under one language. And we will all serve Him.

In Genesis chapters 9 through 11, we are given several examples of sin. And we are given several examples of the consequences. Even a man like Noah could not resist temptation. Neither could Moses or the great King David. No matter how good we have been or how many great things we have done, we are not immune to sin.

> I Corinthians 10:12 *... let him who thinks he stands take heed that he does not fall.*

3) In relation to your walk with God, describe what the above verse means.

_____

_____

_____

_____

_____

The effects of sin are not confined to just the sinner. The sin of adultery obviously affects the marriage and affects the family. The sin of murder obviously affects the victim and affects his family and friends. Some would say that "small sins" are not so bad. They would say that a little "white lie" is necessary sometimes. These "small" sins are very dangerous. There is no excuse for sin. Every sin separates us from God and clearly has affects on others. The every inch that we move away from God is a step closer to Satan. We must keep our focus on God.

Take it to Heart:

We each have a sin nature that is traced back to Adam. There is no denying this sin nature. We can not get rid of it. But, we can recognize it. We can learn to understand the affects the sin nature has on us. A marathon runner will run a race of approximately 26 miles. During the race the runner's body will go through many phases. The legs may start to cramp. The mind may start to wonder and even hallucinate. Dehydration may start to set in. A trained runner strives to recognize the signs of each of the body changes. And a trained runner will compensate when he recognizes the body change. This should be how we understand and handle our sin nature. When our sin nature starts to tempt us in one direction, we need to realize it and double our efforts to focus on God. Just as the runner knows that at mile number 20, his legs always start to cramp, we should know that in certain situations we will not be able to resist temptations. Keep the focus on God.

In your daily walk, name 3 situations that you need to avoid.

How can focusing on God help you through these situations?

Remember even "faithful" Noah could be tempted. **Be strong in God.**

Made in the USA
Columbia, SC
17 September 2024

42394783R00098